Manifest your Everything

Manifest your Everything

love yourself and create your dream life

Nicci Roscoe

CICO BOOKS

LONDON NEW YORK

I dedicate this book to people all over the world who are suffering in any way. Wishing them the opportunity to manifest their everything and find peace, love, and happiness in their life. Sending much love and healing light.

Published in 2023 by CICO Books
An imprint of Ryland Peters & Small Ltd
20–21 Jockey's Fields   341 E 116th St
London WC1R 4BW   New York, NY 10029

www.rylandpeters.com

10 9 8 7 6 5 4 3 2 1

Text © Nicci Roscoe 2023
Design and illustration © CICO Books 2023

Note: Please use caution when performing the exercises in this book. Always consult trained professionals in their fields and follow their advice. The publisher and author cannot accept any responsibility for injury, loss, or damage arising from use of this book.

A CIP catalog record for this book is available from the Library of Congress and the British Library.

ISBN: 978-1-80065-192-0

Printed in China

Illustrator: Camila Gray
Editor: Slav Todorov
Senior designer: Emily Breen
Senior commissioning editor: Carmel Edmonds
Art director: Sally Powell
Creative director: Leslie Harrington
Head of production: Patricia Harrington
Publishing manager: Penny Craig

Contents

Introduction

Showing you how to manifest your everything is one of the most powerful gifts I can give you. Manifesting is asking the universe for what you dream of and focusing on it with positive intent. The universe will hear and you will receive your wishes. When I first opened my eyes following a brain tumor operation I was disorientated and in pain. Out of this confused state I realized that waking up from my operation was what I had manifested. I was so happy and grateful!

Learning how to love myself again and manifest my dreams gave me my life back. I was also told that I may never talk again and could be paralyzed down the right side of my body. Luckily, neither of these things happened and the only debilitating infliction I was left with was chronic pain in the left side of my head and I also have three bolts and six screws. Apparently, one of the screws is loose! But managing pain physically, mentally, emotionally, or spiritually is possible. When you take control of the pain, the universe knows and is open to sending you more ways to help you achieve what you want.

The most exciting thing about writing this book for you is knowing how empowering the "Manifest Your Everything" process is. I've experienced everything I have written about and have also watched my students and clients go through this incredible journey in my "Love Yourself and Manifest Your Dreams" workshops. They feel lighter and full of hope to move forward with their lives. By making this journey they've discovered that it is possible to be free again, find love, believe in themselves, feel peaceful, be grateful for all they have, and live a life full of abundance and happiness.

I'm so delighted to bring you this book which is full of everything you need to know to manifest your everything by letting go of what's holding you back through acceptance and acknowledgment of your situation. Learn to love yourself again, feel confident, courageous, and full of self-compassion and commitment to positive change, so you can create your dream life—the universe will hear you and send you what you wish for.

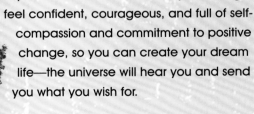

After letting go of what no longer served me and having the positive focus and intent to heal and love myself, I then focused on manifesting good health. The universe heard me and sent me the most precious gift of all: life. I felt a huge release and lighter, with a renewed energy and in control of my emotions. When you hold onto negative emotions, they cause blockages in the body. By releasing them you can open your heart to loving yourself, focus on new beginnings, and get ready to manifest your dreams.

This was my inspiration for helping you to manifest your everything: by showing you the empowering exercises and process I worked through and developed into an exciting journey of positive change. Your journey in this book is full of exercises for you to do, along with different case studies of people who have been through the process, manifested their dreams, and received what they asked for from the universe.

The journey includes letting go of any hurt, anger, or upset that you have been holding onto before saying goodbye with a powerful burning ceremony and cutting the cord for a final release. You then learn how to love yourself through self-care, working with crystals, essential oils, the power of meditation, laughter, smiling, and so much more!

Manifesting when you are coming from a place of peace, calm, and happiness, and having a beautiful feeling of freedom from an open heart, is an all-powerful and enlightening process. Take your time going through each page, learning how to release what you need to, renew your faith and belief in yourself, and ask to receive what you are dreaming of.

I wish you a journey of extraordinary, empowering, and exciting change that brings you the gifts of life you have longed for. Manifesting your everything comes to you with much love, inspiration, and healing light for a beautiful future.

Nicci xx

chapter 1

Letting Go

The journey of manifesting starts with letting go. You need to say goodbye to what's been holding you back as you begin a journey to love yourself and manifest your everything.

The good news is that you can achieve anything you want to and manifest your everything—including feeling confident, finding the best possible relationship or job, or whatever it is you're wishing for, whenever you are ready.

There is a special recipe for making the positive changes necessary for you to manifest your everything. This recipe includes three essential ingredients:

1. Wanting to make it happen.

2. Loving yourself.

3. Acknowledging and accepting the changes you need to make.

Once you understand what these essential ingredients are, you can begin the journey that will take you wherever you want to go. It's exciting; it can happen, and you can make it happen!

The First Step: Learn to Love Yourself

HOW DO I BEGIN LOVING MYSELF?

Start by giving yourself permission to like yourself and accept that now is the time for positive change. Acknowledging emotions that have prevented you from living the life you want will begin the process of releasing the blockages you've been holding onto. When you open your mind, body, and spirit to your needs, everything will begin to flow because you'll feel happier, more confident, and more peaceful. This is when the universe will start to hear you and give you what you want.

Trust and believe in yourself and what you can achieve. This doesn't happen overnight. It's a process that will take you on a special journey of releasing, renewing, and receiving to manifest what you now want in your life.

> "You, yourself, as much as anybody in the entire universe, deserve your love and affection."
>
> Buddha

YOUR JOURNEY TO MANIFESTING YOUR EVERYTHING

- **Release** what doesn't serve you

- **Renew** your faith and belief in you

- **Receive** what you wish for

LIBERATE YOUR MIND

Self-care and loving yourself again—or maybe for the first time—will help you begin releasing the blockages that have been holding you back. It's important to listen to your intuition and what your mind and body are telling you. Letting go of what doesn't serve you physically, mentally, and spiritually can be so freeing. Holding onto feelings of frustration, sadness, and grief can be overwhelming and bring up all kinds of negative emotions that you need to let go of.

STOP resisting giving yourself the care and love you need. No one else can take action to make these changes for you. It's your responsibility to choose what you do and when you do it.

STOP playing the blame game and thinking everything's your fault. Repeat to yourself eight times every morning, lunchtime, and evening: "It's not my fault."

START forgiving those who have hurt you. Forgiveness can open pathways toward feeling happy and peaceful, and to opening your heart to new beginnings (see below, page 20).

START looking at what you have achieved and giving yourself the respect that you deserve.

LEARN TO SAY **"NO!"** TO WHAT DOESN'T SERVE YOU

It can be easy to say "yes" to other people and keep repeating detrimental patterns of behavior. Saying "NO" can be so uplifting, and it is also very beneficial to your well-being and personal journey. You may be afraid to say "no" to your boss who keeps you at work all hours. But if you don't say anything, he'll keep doing it. Or perhaps you are being pulled in all directions by your family and you don't have any time for yourself. This process is about you and feeling happier, more in control, and ensuring you take better care of yourself.

If you don't look after you and give yourself love, then how will you have the energy and mental capacity to take care of others or do your job well?

Learn to say "NO!" You'll notice the difference immediately by having more "me time."

EXERCISE:

Acknowledge and Accept Challenging Emotions

The following exercise is designed to help you start acknowledging and accepting the things that are holding you back. By writing down your well-being score next to the words listed below you can begin the healing process. It can be challenging to acknowledge emotions and feelings that you don't want to accept. But when you see them written down in front of you, it can be a huge relief to know that you are taking your first steps toward gaining control of your emotions and making positive change. This realization may bring up different feelings. That is okay. Remember: you're doing this for you.

On a scale of 1–10, with 1 being the lowest and 10 the highest, write your well-being score in the stars below. If you feel something isn't relevant and you don't need to do any work in this area, then score it 10. You may want to photocopy this page and put your scores on the copy instead. You may also want to photocopy this chart and use it in the longer term to record your own experiences.

Once you have completed this exercise you'll be able to see what you need to change—even though you may have known what this is for a long time and have chosen to ignore. Once you begin your journey to manifest your everything—whether it's to feel happy again, meet your ideal partner, or whatever else you desire—it is possible that your perception of what you want may start to change.

Being honest with yourself—and realizing what you don't want—will help you take your next steps toward understanding what you do want.

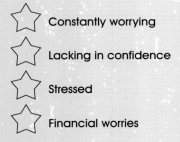

☆ Constantly worrying

☆ Lacking in confidence

☆ Stressed

☆ Financial worries

☆ Lonely

☆ Sad

☆ Angry

☆ Resentful

☆ Upset

☆ Depressed

☆ Afraid

☆ Courageous

☆ Happiness

☆ Peace from within

☆ Relationship with partner

☆ Relationship with family

☆ Relationship with friends

☆ Grieving loss of loved one

☆ Meeting the wrong person
for a relationship

☆ Grieving relationship breakup

☆ Trust in others

☆ Self-worth

☆ Self-trust

☆ Self-belief

☆ Self-perception

☆ Lacking in energy

☆ Sleep

☆ Physical health

☆ Exercise/fitness levels

☆ Nutrition

☆ Mental health

If you wish, please add any other feelings or emotions you think are relevant to you in the spaces below and add your well-being score.

☆ ....

☆ ....

☆ ....

☆ ....

☆ ....

☆ ....

☆ ....

☆ ....

☆ ....

Check to see how your score has improved as you go through the Manifest Your Everything process.

Courage, Confidence, and Self-Worth

Whenever I think of having courage or gaining confidence and self-belief, I always think of the brilliant character of the cowardly lion in the movie *The Wizard of Oz*. Everyone has courage inside them and, just like the lion, it may require a journey along your own yellow brick road to find it and realize that it's always been there.

You can overcome anything you want to—like jumping out of a plane or climbing a mountain!

Your mind is very powerful, and when you focus on taking control, you can find courage within.

Different experiences and situations can influence your beliefs and self-confidence if you let them. These might include not being happy in your job or afraid to tell your boss something important, or perhaps being bullied by a loved one or friend and not having the courage to do something about it because you are afraid of the consequences. The choices you make can take you on an emotional rollercoaster, until you realize that it is possible to make positive changes and do something about your situation.

Your confidence and self-worth can take a huge dip if you don't feel you can say what you want and think that no one is listening. You may feel isolated and that you have no one to give you the comfort you need. Millions of people face dilemmas and situations such as these that they feel they cannot escape. Learning to manage these situations better can help you to:

Give yourself the love, you need.

Take back control of your emotions.

Awaken your strength from within.

Take action and let go of what you know isn't serving you.

Remember, finding the courage, confidence, and self-belief to rediscover your own self-worth will help you create the life you want.

CASE STUDY: A Manifesting Journey

Carly was in a psychologically abusive relationship. When she first met her partner, she had a bubbly personality and she was confident and fun to be around. After being in this relationship for six months she started to notice that her partner was acting differently. He would get upset if she didn't immediately pick up the phone or reply to messages when she was at work or out with a friend. When she got home, he would be waiting for her by the front door to tell her how pathetic and useless she was, and how she would never be good at anything.

Carly was devastated and too embarrassed to tell her family or friends, who thought her partner was lovely. He was good-looking and financially secure. On the outside he appeared to be the perfect companion. He always apologized for treating her badly and showered her with flowers and other gifts, which she accepted, and she forgave him every time. One of Carly's work colleagues noticed she wasn't smiling anymore and looked drawn and tired. One day, everything became too much for her and she broke down and asked her colleague for help. Her friend suggested that she should come to see me.

Breaking away from a relationship you believe is the right one for you can be very hard to do. For whatever reason—however wrong it is—it can be easy to start feeling that everything is your fault.

The good news is that it's not your fault and, after working with Carly, she began to see that it was "his issue"; she was good at what she did and more.

By examining what wasn't right with the relationship and by remembering how she behaved before she met her partner, Carly began to realize what she had allowed him to do. She had lost the bubbly, happy person she once was, and she wanted her back. Carly began the process of letting go. She started loving herself again and found the courage and confidence to end the relationship. **When you say the words: "Enough is enough, I want me back!" out loud to yourself, they can have a very positive effect on how much better you begin to feel**. After a few weeks Carly was ready to make changes in her life, and now had the courage, confidence, and self-belief to do so.

Carly is now in a beautiful relationship which she manifested after letting go of what didn't serve her. She gave herself the love and self-care she needed and is back to being her bubbly, happy self once more.

"Believe you can and you're halfway there."

Theodore Roosevelt

Creating Mental Space

When you're feeling challenged or overwhelmed, it's a good idea to distance yourself mentally from the situation or person causing the problem. The two-part exercise below will help you to imagine whatever is troubling you as being far away rather than holding onto emotions that can make you feel anxious or stressed.

I love this exercise because it's simple and very effective for creating mental space for yourself. You can do it anywhere and at any time, as needed. Do it discreetly and say the words in the steps to yourself instead of out loud if you're with other people.

EXERCISE PART 1: Creating Space

1. Put your left hand on your heart.

2. Say out loud **"I'm taking care of me,"** or say it discreetly to yourself if you're in company.

3. Push your right hand straight out in front of you and focus on it.

4. Imagine you are pushing the person or the situation farther and farther away as you say out loud: **"And you're over there."**

5. Repeat this 8–10 times.

6. Each time you say this, be aware of the space between you and whoever or whatever it is you're "putting over there."

7. Feel yourself relax. Take a slow, deep breath in through your nose and out through your mouth as you release any tension you were holding onto.

EXERCISE PART 2: Gaining Control

1. Put your left hand on your heart.

2. Say out loud **"I'm in control of me—not you,"** or say it discreetly to yourself if you're in company.

3. Push your right hand straight out in front of you and focus on it.

4. Imagine you are pushing the person or the situation farther and farther away as you say out loud: **"This is your issue not mine."**

5. Repeat this 8–10 times.

6. Each time you say this, feel how much more you're gaining control over your emotions.

7. Feel yourself relax and take a slow, deep breath in through your nose and out through your mouth as you release any tension you were holding on to.

What's Holding You Back?

What you tell yourself can have a profound effect on how you feel (see page 90). Perhaps you are afraid to say goodbye to a past relationship? Or are you still upset and angry with a loved one, friend, or family member and not able to forgive them? Perhaps you don't like how you look, and you now need to start accepting that this is you. You are a beautiful person inside and out. The more you let go of negative thoughts, the more you will be able to give yourself what you need.

EXERCISE: **Setting Boundaries**

Stepping out of your comfort zone can be challenging, especially when you are used to being in the same place for a long time. There may be circumstances in a relationship that you are afraid to change. To break out of this situation, try doing the following:

STOP letting others drain you of your energy.

STOP allowing someone to tell you what to do all the time.

START doing what you know is right for you.

If you accept situations that don't serve you and keep sabotaging the good things in your life, nothing will ever change. You may feel you have no confidence or courage to make those changes. But it's important to remember: you can do it!

Tell yourself and others "No more!" and you can find the courage to say what you feel and stand up to your fears. It will help you move forward on your journey to manifesting your everything.

The person who hurt or upset you may never change their behavior. You're the one that needs to make the change.

When you free yourself of the burden of others hurting you and take control it is a wonderful release.

Forgiveness

When you've been hurt by a person or situation you may feel resentment, anger, or bitterness. This can affect your health and behavior in many ways, causing increased anxiety or sleep deprivation. If you hold onto grudges and seek revenge, this can heighten the emotional damage you are doing to yourself. By understanding how forgiveness can offer release from the negative energies you are holding onto, you can work toward letting go and creating peace and calm in your heart. By choosing to forgive the person or situation, you are releasing their control over you instead of being a victim.

REMEMBERING WHAT HAPPENED IS DIFFERENT TO FORGIVING

Forgiving is different to forgetting. It doesn't mean you need to let the person back into your life. This may be a person who is a negative influence or someone who is harmful mentally and/or physically to you or your family. You may never forget the hurt. That's okay. It can be a good protective mechanism to ensure that nothing like this ever happens again. Maintaining a mental distance—especially if you still need to see this person for family reasons or because they are part of your social circle—can give you the strength you need to manage the situation. (See the exercises Creating Space and Gaining Control above.)

Time is an incredible healer. When you go through the letting-go process, it's amazing how quickly you begin to look at things differently and acquire a new perspective.

> "Forgive others, not because they deserve forgiving, but because you deserve peace."
>
> Buddha

Release Inner Turmoil through Meditation

Meditation, exercise, and healthy eating all play a big role in your journey of self-care, loving yourself, and being ready to manifest your everything. Meditation is a wonderful way to clear your mind, give you clarity, and help you feel inner peace and calm. The more you practice meditating, the more you will feel the benefits. Meditation will not only help you control distracting thoughts, but it will also enable you to focus on the positive. You'll then start to feel so much more open to loving yourself. It can help in so many other ways—you may notice that you have much more energy, are sleeping better, and can start giving yourself the self-care you need.

The first time I meditated I was shocked at how powerful silence can be. I now meditate daily for 30 minutes each morning and evening. This may not be practical for you, so find a schedule that works best for you and your lifestyle. There are many ways to meditate, including focusing on your breath, visualization, walking in nature, and listening to music. You can also focus on repeating positive words over and over again, such as "I am letting go of my past and embracing the future and that feels good" or "I feel happy, peaceful, and ready to live my life."

If you haven't meditated before, just start with a few minutes each day, and notice how much better you begin to feel. You can then increase your meditation time as you become more comfortable with the process and feel the positive benefits it has on your life. I suggest meditating for two minutes to begin with. Then build up to five minutes, 10 minutes, 15 minutes, and, finally, 20 minutes or more. It can be helpful to set an alarm on your phone or clock to time your session. You might also like to play some relaxing music or listen to the soothing sounds of nature.

EXERCISE 1: How to Meditate

1. Sit in an upright position on a chair, sofa, or bed with the palms of your hands facing up and resting on your thighs.

2. Close your eyes or focus on one area in your room or outside a window, such as the leaves on a tree.

3. Relax your neck and shoulders and imagine a piece of string from the top of your head gently pulling you up to the sky, so that your spine is straight.

4. Take a slow, deep breath in through your nose for a count of 4 and then slowly release through your mouth for a count of 5. Repeat this three times.

5. Now find a comfortable breath pattern for you and breathe normally.

6. Focus on saying to yourself: "I feel calm, peaceful, and relaxed."

7. Keep repeating these words. If anything else comes into your mind, allow it to flow out and keep coming back to your words. The more you say these words, the more they will go into your unconscious mind.

8. Now take a slow, deep breath in through your nose and then slowly out through your mouth three times.

9. Gently open your eyes and take a minute or so to embrace how you are feeling.

EXERCISE 2: Connecting with Nature

Smell the roses. Let nature connect with your inner being to nurture, nourish, and heighten your senses. When you succumb to the powers of nature, there is a part of you that will begin to feel free and peaceful. Nature is nurturing and will nourish your soul. It provides comfort and a sense of peace in challenging times and can turn sadness into a smile, soothing you into a positive state of feeling contented and free.

Daily walks by the sea, or in big, open country spaces, can help reduce stress levels, boost the immune system, and ease aches and pains. Just breathing in sea or country air is like being given a natural boost of energy.

Every time I teach my "Love Yourself and Manifest Your Dreams" workshop, I always begin by giving everyone a single rose. I ask them to allow any thoughts that may arise to float out of the window—just for this moment—and to focus on their beautiful rose while they inhale its wonderful fragrance. Just stopping and taking the time to enjoy the fragrance of a rose can give you a sense of calm and peace. There is a beautiful life out there just waiting for you to embrace and live it again, exactly how you want to!

EXERCISE 3: Crystal Meditation for Letting Go

The following meditation is best done with a eudialyte crystal. If you don't have this crystal at hand, you can focus on a picture of it and imagine holding it instead. Crystals give you what you need through their unique energy and vibrations. This crystal is wonderful for helping you to let go. I can feel its vibrations and power in my hands every time I hold it.

1. Think about the areas of your life that you wrote down on pages 12–13.

2. Hold the eudialyte crystal in your right hand.

3. Sit in an upright position on a chair, sofa, or bed with the palms of your hands facing up and resting on your thighs.

4. Close your eyes or focus on one area in your room or outside a window, such as the leaves on a tree.

5. Relax your neck and shoulders and imagine a piece of string running from the top of your head gently pulling you up to the sky, so your spine is nice and straight.

6. Take a slow, deep breath in through your nose for the count of 4 and then slowly release through your mouth for a count of 5. Repeat this three times.

7. Now find a comfortable breath pattern for you and breathe normally.

8. Imagine there is a golden light at the center of your heart, and that this golden light is flowing out in all directions.

9. Feel the warmth of the light and see different shades of gold, yellow, and orange.

10. Feel or imagine the crystal sitting in your hand.

11. Now think of one of the areas you have been holding onto and give yourself permission to let go.

12. See this leaving your body as it begins to flow out from your heart into the golden light and become tiny specks.

13. As the light begins to flow through your body and out through areas such as your throat, ears, fingertips, or toes, see the tiny specks leave and disappear into the universe.

14. Feel the release and slowly take a deep breath in through your nose and then slowly out through your mouth as you experience the golden light shining even brighter, knowing you have been letting go of what no longer serves you.

15. Take another breath in and release, then open your eyes and smile!

16. Now you have done this you can do the same with others areas you are holding on to and give yourself permission to let go.

Remarkable Trees

Trees are truly magnificent. They have so much to give, whether they are standing alone or in a circle, and they represent so many things, including strength, love, and grounding. As trees stand tall with their branches swaying in the wind, you can hear them communicating with each other—it's as if they're whispering and know you are there! At other times, they're silent and still, as if they're sleeping.

Many years ago, when I was a teenager, I found it amusing when people said that they hugged trees. After hugging one myself, I didn't laugh anymore; I loved the sense of calm and connection I felt. I then discovered the power of meditation by placing my hands on a tree I felt drawn to. This gave me the peace I was looking for, and I wanted to share this wonderful feeling with my clients and students.

I was fortunate to live near a stunning circle of trees and loved walking into the center to feel their amazing energy. Other people I took with me chose a tree to help them focus their meditation. My grandson Louis had his first experience in the circle of trees when he was two and loved playing inside the circle. He naturally went to his favorite tree and put his hands on it. This was a very special moment.

CASE STUDY: The Nature Cure (Matty's Story)

Matty's profound experience is something he will always remember. He was holding onto a lot of resentment and anger. It was raining heavily on the day we visited the circle of trees and he had brought a very large, bright red golf umbrella with him.

I asked him which tree he was drawn to, and he went straight to the grandmother tree that overlooks the others. To him it represented strength, life, and freedom. He balanced his umbrella on the tree branches, so he could stand underneath it. The rain began to fall even more heavily and Matty suddenly walked into the center of the trees, without his umbrella, extended his arms up toward the universe and said out loud: "I'm free."

The rain and the wind made him feel wonderful. Something in him was liberated that day. It was so magical and beautiful to see. Since my visit to the circle of trees with him, he has been going there regularly to meditate. This part of the process—when he was working with me—was an integral part of Matty's journey of letting go and manifesting what he wanted.

Rituals for Letting Go

Letting go is a process of releasing mentally painful or hurtful emotions that you have been holding on to. These may be negative memories or present situations you need to free yourself from to enable you to move on in your life. It may be a person or a situation that has left you feeling vulnerable, angry, or lacking self-worth and confidence.

For this three-part exercise you'll need several sheets of letter-size (A4) paper, a ruler, pen or pencil, a pair of scissors, shell dish (preferably abalone) or fireproof dish, and some matches or a barbecue lighter, as well as good ventilation (an open window) and a kitchen sink with running water. You'll also need a piece of cord that's easy to cut in half.

Part 1 of this exercise gives you the opportunity to write down everything you want to let go of to begin your releasing process.

EXERCISE PART 1: Setting Your Intention

Setting your intention to focus on freeing yourself from the emotions you are holding on to will begin the process of letting go and giving you peace in your heart and space to breathe again in your mind. Be brave, honest, and truthful with yourself. Ask the question "Do these thoughts and feelings serve me by holding on to them?" Writing down everything you wish to free yourself from can be emotional and often a surprise as to how much you need to let go of!

1. Using the letter-size (A4) paper in landscape, draw 6 lines down and 4 lines across the page to give you about 35 equally-sized squares to write on. Use as many sheets as you need.

2. Write the things you want to let go of in each square on the pieces of paper. These might be people or situations that have hurt or scared you, or the emotions caused by certain circumstances or relationships. Take your time. You may have been holding onto these issues for a long time and might feel very emotional when you write them down.

EXERCISE PART 2: **Saying Goodbye with a Burning Ceremony**

The burning ceremony is a powerful ritual of saying goodbye to the negative emotions you have held onto. As you see your papers burn to ashes and you smell the embers it is confirmation that a new chapter of your life is about to begin. Tell yourself "That was then, this is now! I'm free!"

Safety Warning: keep away from children. All burning needs to be done in the sink with the window open. It's not to be done without ventilation. Running water must be available too. The burning ceremony can also be done outside in a safe area.

1. Once you have written down everything you want to say goodbye to, cut each square out one at a time and focus on what it says for a few seconds. Fold each piece of paper several times, so you are left with lots of tiny pieces of paper.

2. Place all the pieces of paper in the shell dish or other fireproof dish that won't be damaged by fire.

3. Now put the dish containing all the pieces of paper in the sink (or you can do this outside in a safe area).

4. Open the window, then start lighting the papers and watch the flames as they burn.

5. Let go of everything you have carried with you that's been painful, anything that has hurt or frightened you, or any emotions you have felt toward a situation or a person that you are now saying goodbye to.

6. Different emotions may come up for you as you're doing this. These are natural and all part of the letting-go process. Be kind to yourself and give yourself time to process what you are doing.

7. While the papers are burning, repeat to yourself: **"I am letting you go now to give myself a new life filled with love and all I wish for. I have carried you for too long. This is goodbye! It feels so good. I am free, I am happy, I am peaceful. Thank you."**

8. Now run tepid water over the smoldering paper and say your final goodbyes. If you are doing the burning ceremony outside, please take a large bottle of water with you to pour over the burned ashes.

9. You can throw these ashes away or bury them in the earth, so they will be reborn to good purpose, sending positive messages to the universe.

EXERCISE PART 3: **Cutting the Cord**

The final part of your letting-go ceremony is cutting the cord. By doing this you're finally cutting all ties to what was—and opening your heart to all the good things you are now ready to embrace and manifest.

1. Cut a piece of cord about 15 in. (40 cm) in length. If you are on your own, you may want to make the cord longer and tie one end to a chair or door handle.

2. Pull hard on the other end of the cord and then cut at the central point to feel complete release.

3. If someone is with you, they can cut the cord for you. Hold either end of the cord in your hands and pull very tight. Take a deep breath in and release out as your friend cuts the cord in the center. This gives you a wonderful feeling of release as you finally let go and say "goodbye."

If a situation arises that you feel you want to let go of, then repeat the burning ceremony followed by cutting the cord. You can do this whenever you feel it is necessary.

Once You've Said Goodbye: Meditations and Rituals

When you've said your final goodbye it's time to give yourself the love and care you need. Replace what you have let go of by focusing on good intentions of love to fill your mind and body with the beauty and energy of crystal love during this meditation.

MEDITATION TO GIVE YOU BACK THE LOVE

You will need a morganite crystal to fill you with love and to replace what you have let go of with all your good intentions, or you can focus on the picture on this page. Once you have completed the burning ceremony (see page 27), either hold the morganite crystal in your left hand or focus on the picture shown here and imagine holding it in the palm of your left hand.

1. Hold or imagine the morganite crystal in your left hand ready to receive love.

2. Sit in an upright position on a chair, sofa, or bed with the palms of your hands facing up and resting on your thighs.

3. Relax your neck and shoulders and imagine a piece of string gently pulling you up from the top of your head to the sky.

4. Close your eyes or focus on one area in the room or outside a window, such as the leaves on a tree.

5. Take a slow, deep breath in through your nose for a count of 4 and then slowly release through your mouth for a count of 5. Repeat this three times.

6. Now find a comfortable breath pattern for you and breathe normally.

7. Feel or imagine the crystal in your hand. Breathe in the gentle pink color of this stone that is full of love and good intentions.

8. Allow the aroma of the stone to flow up your nose, into your head, and down through your throat, filling the space in your heart with this beautiful, calm, peaceful love.

9. Feel the peacefulness within you and see it washing over you.

10. Remain in this calming state of meditation and love for 2–5 minutes.

11. Take a deep breath in through your nose and release slowly from your mouth.

12. Open your eyes and refocus your attention back into the room.

13. Hold the morganite crystal, or imagine it in your hand, and give thanks to the universe for the love and peace you are now feeling.

CLEANSING YOUR HOME, YOURSELF, AND OTHERS

Following the burning ceremony and meditation (see pages 27 and 29), I suggest cleansing key areas in your home to protect you and keep your living space free of negativity. Once you've done this, you'll notice the difference. There will be a sense of peace and calm, and the scent of the sage used in the cleansing can also be very relaxing.

Sage has been used for centuries to cleanse and protect. It's part of an ancient ceremony that the American First Nation People have always done and is known as a "smudging ceremony." When you smudge, you cleanse. You can either cleanse every room in your home, or just where you feel it is needed.

EXERCISE: **The Smudging Ceremony**

Doing your own smudging ceremony gives an amazing sense of release, calm and peace to your home, yourself, and others. You'll need a sage bundle (these are available for purchase), a shell dish (preferably an abalone shell dish to collect the ash from the burning bundle), a large feather, and a ventilated room if you are working inside. Please note that this ceremony is traditionally done outside. If you're smudging the inside of a house or workspace, the windows must be open.

1.   Light one end of the sage bundle and then blow out the flame to enable the smoke to circulate.

2.   Make sure to place the shell dish underneath the bundle as it begins to burn. The dish is meant to catch the ashes, so they don't damage the floor or other surface. For this ancient ceremony the shell dish is one of the four elements (Earth, Air, Fire, and Water), below:

   •   The shell represents water

   •   The sage represents earth

   •   The smoke represents fire

   •   The feather represents air *and carries your prayers to spirit*

3.   Use the feather to direct the smoke over whatever you are cleansing. Hold the sage bundle in one hand over the shell dish and waft the smoke with your feather in the other hand.

   •   If you're doing the smudging ceremony on yourself, waft the smoke around you with the feather. Start from the top of your head, go down one side of your body, then the other, and finally down the center.

   •   If you're smudging someone else, ask them to stand with their arms outstretched and legs one hip's width apart. Smudge from the top of the head down the center, front and back, and then each side, under the arms and the outside and inside of each leg.

4.   Feel the change in the room you have cleansed as the smoke wafts out of the window.

5.   Repeat this exercise as often as feels necessary. Use your intuition to tell you if a room needs a "smudging ceremony."

EXERCISE: **Ground Yourself and Reconnect with the Earth**

There may be times when you may feel dizzy or light-headed or unable to focus mentally or physically. By performing this grounding ritual, you are rebalancing your mind and body and reconnecting with the Earth, which will help you focus and feel more level-headed. Imagine doing the following exercise whenever you feel you need to ground yourself.

1. Stand barefoot in the grass and imagine you have roots growing from the soles of your feet deep into the ground, attaching themselves to a beautiful, golden light. Feel yourself grounding as your mind and body are now so much more centered.

2. Hold a hematite crystal in your hands whenever you feel the need for extra support to feel more grounded.

PROTECTION RITUAL

From the moment you walk out the front door, make sure you're protected. You can be walking down the street or sitting in a coffee shop and still pick up the negative energy and emotions emanating from passers-by. Protect yourself every day by doing the following:

1. Visualize—imagine you have a beautiful purple, pink, or golden light around you.

2. Tell yourself: "I am protected."

3. Wear a tourmaline, turquoise, or aquamarine crystal as a pendant or bracelet, or carry a piece of tourmaline with you.

Turquoise and aquamarine are also wonderful crystals to wear to protect you when traveling. You might be going on holiday, to the shops, or to work. Wherever you travel turquoise and aquamarine are special companions.

IN SUMMARY: Tips to Remember

1. Remember to laugh! It's a wonderful alternative medicine.

2. Meditate to help clear your mind.

3. Remind yourself of what you want.

4. Feel courage and strength deep within.

5. Remember to say "NO!"

6. Feel the benefits of forgiveness.

7. Release anything that doesn't serve you by performing the burning ceremony (see page 27).

8. Stay grounded and centered (see page 32).

9. Protect yourself every day (see page 32).

10. Love yourself.

YOUR GUIDE TO HAVING COURAGE

Confidence will give you the power to speak out, feel positive, and be happy.

Optimism gives you the hope and peace of mind to know everything's going to be okay.

Universe: the universe hears you and manifests your dreams.

Resilience is knowing that nothing is going to hold you back.

Action: take action to do what is right for you and don't be afraid anymore.

Giving yourself the love you deserve.

Empowerment gives you strength and positive energy from within.

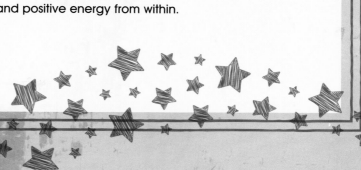

chapter 2

Giving Yourself Love

Now you have said goodbye to what doesn't serve you after doing the exercises in Chapter 1 Letting Go, it's time to start giving yourself love and taking care of your needs and well-being. Life will begin to flow in many ways. Your outlook on everything can change as you begin to feel healthier and more confident and stronger from within—and ready to enjoy the life you want to create.

Listen to your heart, mind, and body when they're telling you that they need to be nurtured and cared for. By tuning in to your intuition, you'll know that it's okay to say "No" to what doesn't serve you and "Yes" to giving yourself what you need. This will open pathways that send the right messages to the universe and help raise your positive vibrations. Your mind and body will feel more grounded, peaceful, and calm.

Start taking some time to give yourself the love you deserve. Stop coming up with excuses as to why you can't—and tell yourself that you can.

"Let me take some time each day to look within the self and experience the beauty of my inner qualities."

Brahma Kumaris

What Do You Love About You?

Focusing on the good things about yourself can help boost your confidence and self-worth. The more you focus on negative language, the longer you'll send your unconscious mind messages that won't help you. Tell yourself:

"I am a beautiful person inside and out."

Start believing this! Start loving the beautiful you! You may find this challenging at first, but keep doing it! Continuous practice—or, as I like to call it, the three "P's"—is essential, so remember to Practice, Practice, Practice! Repeat again:

"I am a beautiful person inside and out."

EXERCISE PART 1: **Getting Started**

By doing this exercise you'll be sending positive messages to the universe, and the universe will respond with what you are wishing for. If you're continuously thinking about what you don't like about yourself and your life, you'll be sending out the wrong message and continue to receive what you don't want.

1. Slowly take a deep breath in through your nose, and as you do so, breathe in belief, love, and positivity. See, feel, or hear the words floating into your mind and body.

2. Slowly breathe out through your mouth, letting any negative thoughts or beliefs flow out of your mind. Feel your shoulders relax as you do this.

3. Repeat steps 1 and 2 three times.

4. Find a comfortable breath for you and breathe normally.

5. Now place your hand on your heart and repeat these words out loud eight times: **"I believe in me."**

6. Keep saying this with more conviction each time and you'll begin to feel it.

EXERCISE PART 2: **Celebrate Your Qualities**

1. In the first box below, write your caring qualities such as "I am kind," "I am empathetic," and "I am loving."

2. Then, write your creative qualities in the next box, such as playing a musical instrument, singing, dancing, painting, designing, writing poetry, carpentry, sculpting models with clay—the possibilities are endless.

3. In the third box write what you are proud of achieving. This could be anything from high school and life-long learning, such as sporting, artistic, or academic achievements—at school, at home, at work, or at play. Here, think about what you have achieved in life and not what you haven't done.

"What you think, you become.
What you feel, you attract.
What you imagine, you create."

Buddha

My caring qualities are:

My creative qualities are:

Things I'm proud of achieving are:

EXERCISE PART 3: **Celebrate Your Appearance**

1. Look at yourself in a full-length mirror.

2. What are your favorite features? Write these down. Maybe you love your hair or your eyes. If you don't like a certain part of your body, such as your bottom or your nose, change your perception and tell yourself "It's okay"—and that you love yourself just the way you are.

STOP comparing yourself to others. **STOP** listening to negativity from others. It's easy to let them into your head if you're feeling vulnerable. Take control! You can choose what you think and feel, and what you say to yourself. If a family member or friend is going through a tough time, avoid letting them drain your energy. Being supportive is fine, but you don't have to take on their "issues."

Now is the time to focus on yourself and be kind to you. You may not think you have the perfect nose, bottom, or figure. But you are the perfect you!

It's the positive words you tell yourself that will help you feel good. What you say and how you learn to manage different situations will have a positive impact on your outlook. When you start realizing this, the universe will hear you. It will keep sending you the courage and confidence you are wishing for.

Just one small positive thought in the morning can change your whole day."

Dalai Lama

Loving and Nurturing Yourself

Giving yourself love may be something you've never done before, or perhaps have forgotten how to do. When I was in hospital for a long time following an operation, a friend sent me a gift of rose-scented hand cream. I was unable to have the television or radio on at the time, and needed a focus to give myself some nurturing. Every day for the next few weeks I gave my hands a slow massage with this beautiful cream. It felt calming, soothing, and comforting. When I left hospital, I continued massaging the cream into my hands every day and it became a part of my daily meditation.

EXERCISE: Hand Cream Meditation

This is a wonderful meditation to show yourself love and self-care.

1. Find a hand cream you love the smell of and that is easily absorbed. Rose is special for me. The scent is so calming and immediately makes me feel relaxed. There may be a particular fragrance that you love, like lavender or fruits such as nectarine, strawberries, or passion fruit. It's important to find the right one for you.

2. Sit somewhere comfortable and listen to some calm, peaceful music, or let silence be your calm.

3. Put some cream on your hands and slowly massage your palms and then the backs of your hands.

4. Any time your mind starts to wander—perhaps thinking about your shopping list or what you're going to have for dinner—keep coming back to focus on your hands.

5. Start to slowly massage each finger and fingertip, focusing on each one individually.

6. Take a slow, deep breath in through your nose and then slowly out through your mouth. Repeat this three times.

Being the Authentic You

One of my favorite movies about being authentic is *Legally Blonde* starring Reese Witherspoon, who plays the aspiring lawyer Elle Woods. Elle loves her life, her friends, and her boyfriend Warner Huntingdon III. She is expecting him to propose. He shatters her dreams by telling her that he needs to choose someone more serious for his future career in politics. Warner has applied to Harvard University. He makes her feel worthless and stupid. Elle is devastated.

With a positive attitude, determination, and support from her friends, Elle decides that she isn't going to let this get her down anymore. She focuses on getting Warner back and applies to Harvard herself. She doesn't change any of her fun, characteristic ways. It is refreshing to see the surprised gentleman on the admissions board agree to accept her pink, scented application form.

The message from this movie is that by being the authentic you and focusing on positive outcomes, you can achieve anything you want—with any color paper, from pink to sky blue!

Sometimes you may think you know what you want. And it can take courage and focus to come to your senses and suddenly realize that the person or job you thought was right for you actually isn't. In *Legally Blonde*, Elle realizes that Warner isn't the one for her. Everything was about his needs. She also discovers what an amazing lawyer she could be and embarks on her new career with excitement, professionalism, and care. Elle retains her fun-loving, positive self.

So, being the authentic you, and trusting and believing in yourself, can give you the confidence and happiness you have been searching for. Never change yourself for anyone. Don't try to please another person if it doesn't feel right. Start giving yourself the love and self-care you need.

Elle Woods loved spending time at the beauty salon having her nails done. Remember what you love doing too and just do it!

What is Self-Care?

Self-care is essential to your well-being. The Circle of Self-Care (see page 42) is designed to provide inspiration and give you the opportunity to begin taking care of yourself. You need to start taking steps to do things you have avoided for a long time. Any of the ideas below, some of which are taken from the Circle of Self-Care, can have a very positive impact on your well-being and give you a feel-good factor because you are looking after and loving yourself:

- **Pamper yourself.** When was the last time you really pampered yourself and had a day of pure indulgence, giving yourself a facial, having a massage, or going to the gym?

- **Meditate and relax.** Meditating is a wonderful way to relax and clear your mind. The Hand Cream Meditation (see page 39) is just one example you could try. There are so many ways to meditate, including visualization, listening to music, focusing on your breathing, and much more. (See Release Inner Turmoil Through Meditation on page 21 for some more soothing meditation exercises.)

- **Have fun and laugh.** When was the last time you laughed and had fun with a friend or loved one? Laughter releases endorphins, which are your body's natural feel-good chemicals. It's a wonderful way to help you refocus and heal emotional wounds. Laughing has numerous other benefits, including boosting the immune system. It's great for releasing stress and decreasing pain. Make time to bring laughter back into your life and have some fun.

- **See family and friends.** Spending quality time with family and friends may be something you have wanted to do for a long time. Maybe you have missed the personal contact and feeling of love you receive from them. Are you ready to heal old wounds with loved ones and enjoy their company once more?

- **Be creative.** Perhaps you have been wanting to get creative and start painting or singing classes. There are numerous possibilities.

What Are You Doing to Take Care of Yourself?

You can create your own Circle of Self-Care, which is all about you and giving yourself the love and nurturing you need.

EXERCISE PART 1: Create Your Circle of Self-Care

1. Photocopy the circle on this page, so you can fill it in.

2. Look at each section in turn and think of words connected to that theme which are important to you. This will help you to start focusing on what you can do to take care of yourself and your needs. Write these words in each section.

3. Once the circle is complete, you could create your own Circle of Self-Care and add different sections that resonate with you.

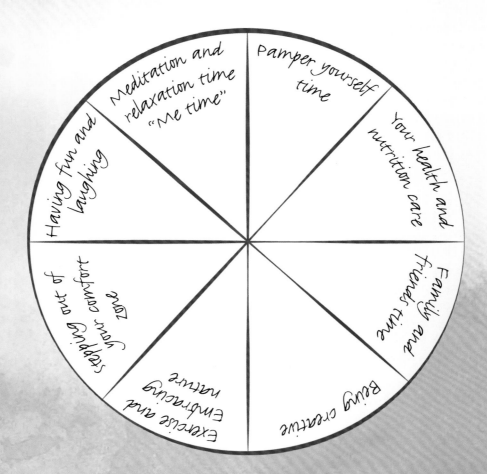

EXERCISE PART 2: **Use Your Circle of Self-Care with Crystal Love**

Crystals know what you need and continue to send their powerful healing energy and vibrations for days after you have worked with them. Follow these next steps to bring crystals into your Circle of Self-Care (see overleaf and page 46 on selecting crystals). Each section of your circle is important. The crystals will know this and enhance whatever is needed. Each crystal has many meanings. I have focused on one crystal to go with each section in your Circle of Self-Care.

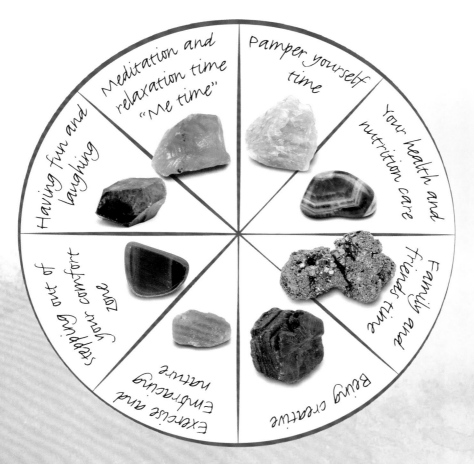

CRYSTALS FOR YOUR CIRCLE OF SELF-CARE

There are lots of crystals available that can provide you with what you need. Below are some suggestions for common crystals and how they can influence your emotions and help you deal with different situations:

TIGER'S EYE
Courage

RHODOCHROSITE
Passion

AMETHYST
Spiritual awakening

GARNET
Energy

CITRINE
New beginnings

BLUE LACE AGATE
Saying what you feel

QUARTZ CRYSTAL
Overall healing

CHALCEDONY
Childhood and past experiences

ROSE QUARTZ
Love

PYRITE
Abundance

ORANGE CALCITE
Laughter

AVENTURINE
Success

GREEN CALCITE
Calm

TOURMALINE
Protection

CRAZY LACE AGATE
Confidence

USING A PENDULUM WITH YOUR CIRCLE OF SELF-CARE

1. Ask your pendulum a question just once, and only about the present. It won't tell you what's in the future.

2. You can ask your pendulum to tell you which crystal to choose for each section of the circle when you hold your pendulum over your crystals. Everyone's "yes" and "no" answers may be different. Your pendulum may go backward and forward for "yes" and in a circular motion for "no." Someone else's may do the opposite. Both are right.

3. Focus on your Circle of Self-Care one section at a time. Start with the first section for which you would like to choose a crystal, such as "Having Fun and Laughing."

4. Now hold your pendulum over one of the crystals you are drawn to and ask "Is this crystal for my 'Having Fun and Laughing' section in my Circle of Self-Care?" If your pendulum tells you "yes," then that is the crystal to put there. If it tells you "no," then keep asking your pendulum about each crystal until you find the one for the first section.

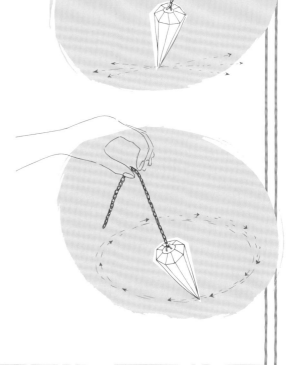

5. Repeat step 4 for each section until they all contain one crystal. The more you practice this, the better you will become as you awaken your natural intuition.

6. Once you have finished choosing your crystals, leave your Circle of Self-Care with your crystals in place somewhere safe and out of reach from tiny hands or pets.

7. Leave your Circle of Self-Care until you feel that you have achieved everything written in each section.

8. Continue to work with your Circle of Self-Care and add different sections to it that resonate with you.

CHOOSING CRYSTALS FOR YOUR CIRCLE OF SELF-CARE

You will need to choose a crystal for each of the eight sections in your circle. Your intuition is powerful, but sometimes you may choose to ignore what it is telling you. It's always right! Listen to it. Choosing a crystal for each section is as simple as listening to your intuition. But you may need a little help to reassure you. A pendulum can provide that help and direction. Working with a pendulum reflects what you know already and is reaffirming. I love seeing the joy and surprise on my students' faces when their pendulum gives them the answer they knew all along.

Dowsing has been practiced for thousands of years. It's fascinating and wonderful that you can obtain the answers you need. Cavemen used sticks to find water underground. They held a forked stick out in front of them while walking along until it moved up or down to show them where the water was. Dowsing rods work on a similar principle. Working with a crystal pendulum is a lot simpler, more practical, and it's easier to carry with you. You'll also have the added benefit of a beautiful crystal at the end of your pendulum chain.

EXERCISE: Working with Crystals and Chakras

Give yourself a self-healing treatment with the crystals in your Circle of Self-Care. This can help you to unblock and rebalance your chakras and provide you with what you need. This exercise shows you how to choose a crystal from the sections in your Circle of Self-Care for each of your seven chakras, leaving one left over to hold.

1. Use your pendulum to ask each crystal in one section at a time: "Is this crystal for my Crown chakra?" If it says "yes" put this aside for your Crown chakra. If your pendulum says "no," then ask if it is for your Brow chakra and so on until you have a crystal from each section for the seven chakras.

2. Once you have selected all seven crystals, lie down somewhere comfortable and place the correct crystal on each of the chakras, from your Base to your Crown. The crystals in this exercise are intended to re-balance the chakras.

3. Hold the eighth crystal from your Circle of Self-Care in your left hand for receiving love.

4. Set an alarm for 5–10 minutes, close your eyes and relax, and then remove the crystals one at a time.

WHAT ARE CHAKRAS?

Chakras are energy "hot spots" focused in specific areas that run down the center line of your body from your head to the base of your spine. There are varying numbers of chakras in different Eastern traditions. We're going to focus on the seven major chakras traditionally used in the West. Sometimes these balls of energy become blocked. By giving yourself a healing treatment with crystals (see Working with Crystals and Chakras, opposite), you can unblock these energy balls, which will help you to feel so much better.

Although the chakras are focused in the center of the body, they are also the hot spots where your energy connects with the outside world. These energy hot spots are bigger than your physical body, emerging as an energy field aura that surrounds your body.

These are the seven major chakras, from the top of the head to the base of the spine:

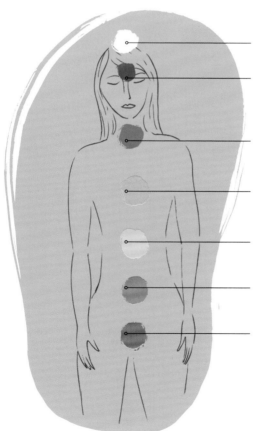

7. Crown: Top of the head

6. Brow: Middle of the forehead (sometimes known as the Third Eye)

5. Throat: Base of the throat

4. Heart: Center of the chest

3. Solar plexus: Just under the breastbone

2. Sacral: Just below the belly button

1. Base: In line with the base of the spine

Heighten Your Senses, Relax, and Rejuvenate

You can use the beautiful fragrance of essential oils to heighten your senses and produce a positive effect on difficult emotions or issues, including anxiety, resolution, and confidence. Just inhaling the fragrance from these concentrated plant extracts can give you a therapeutic boost.

There are so many ways to use essential oils such as having an aromatherapy massage or putting a few drops in your bath water. You can also put some drops in an aromatherapy diffuser to add a delightful fragrance to the space you're in to tap into your senses. This may be at home, at work, or anywhere you want to create a therapeutic atmosphere. An aromatherapy diffuser can also help improve sleep and enhance your mood, depending on the essential oils used.

You can also restore yourself by indulging in a crystal bath (that is: a bath with added crystals) for a rejuvenating self-treatment. You can also add a few drops of essential oil to your crystal bath. Combining crystals and essential oils can be incredibly powerful as you absorb both their energies. (See also Cleansing Crystals, page 141.)

Here are a few suggestions for crystal baths with essential oils to manifest different moods and effects. I always recommend using tumble polished stones because they don't scratch the bath—or you! Naturally rough stones will have the same effect, but if you do decide to use them, be careful not to scratch the bath as you put them in. It's important to choose the crystals that resonate with you. If you're not sure which crystal to choose, use dowsing to help you decide (see Choosing Crystals for Your Circle of Self-Care, page 46).

USING ESSENTIAL OILS

Diluting essential oils with a carrier oil will protect your skin and your well-being, enabling you to benefit from these oils in a safe and effective way. If you're not sure how to use essential oils, ask a qualified aromatherapy practitioner for advice. Never apply undiluted essential oils directly to the skin as they are very potent and quickly absorbed by the body. Always blend them with a carrier oil such as fractionated coconut oil, sweet almond oil, jojoba oil, or olive oil (see page 55).

Safety warning: Never use essential oils without consulting a qualified aromatherapist if you are pregnant or have any significant medical conditions. This isn't a complete list, but essential oils such as clary sage, rose, and lavender should never be used during pregnancy. Please be extremely careful when using any essential oils on children or the elderly. Check with a professional who knows!

TIME FOR YOU

Taking the time to give yourself what you need is essential to your well-being and good health. Planning a date in your diary with yourself can benefit you so much and give you back the positive energy and focus you need. Just thinking about doing something won't change anything. Taking action will! And that's when you begin to see and feel the results.

ROSE QUARTZ BATH FOR LOVE

Relaxing in a rose quartz bath is so therapeutic, soothing, and calming. Rose quartz is the crystal for love. You can feel the loving crystal energy as you step into your bath. When you add drops of rose essential oil, this heightens your senses and opens your heart to giving yourself even more love.

YOU WILL NEED

Small bag of tumble polished rose quartz stones, good-quality pure rose essential oil, carrier oil of choice (such as fractionated coconut oil, sweet almond oil, or jojoba oil), bath filled with water at a temperature you prefer, rose-scented body lotion or massage oil (optional)

1. Cleanse the rose quartz stones under water for a minute before adding them to the bath.

2. Add 5–10 drops of rose essential oil blended with a tablespoon of carrier oil to the bath water.

3. Lie back in the bath to enjoy the aroma of the rose oil and the relaxing feeling produced by the rose quartz crystals.

4. Following your bath, use a rose-scented body lotion or massage oil to complete your loving-yourself treatment. When massaging essential oil into your skin, it's important to blend it with a carrier oil (see Using Essential Oils, page 49).

TIGER'S EYE BATH FOR COURAGE

Using a powerful blend of tiger's eye and bergamot essential oil in your bath will leave you feeling motivated and inspired to stop being afraid and start taking action! Bergamot essential oil, which is very uplifting and light with a citrus aroma, is the perfect oil to add to give you courage and a boost of confidence.

YOU WILL NEED

Small bag of tumble polished tiger's eye stones, good-quality pure bergamot essential oil, carrier oil of choice (such as fractionated coconut oil, sweet almond oil, or jojoba oil), bath filled with water at a temperature you prefer

1. Cleanse the tiger's eye stones under water for a minute before adding them to the bath.

2. Add 5–10 drops of bergamot essential oil blended with a tablespoon of carrier oil to the bath water.

3. Lie back in the bath to enjoy the aroma of the bergamot oil and the feeling of courage created by the oil and tiger's eye stones.

CRAZY LACE AGATE BATH FOR CONFIDENCE

For this crystal and essential oil bath treatment, use the confidence-boosting powers of crazy lace agate and ylang ylang essential oil.

YOU WILL NEED

Small bag of tumble polished crazy lace agate stones, good-quality pure ylang ylang essential oil, carrier oil of choice (such as fractionated coconut oil, sweet almond oil, or jojoba oil), bath filled with water at a temperature you prefer

1. Cleanse the crazy lace agate stones under water for a minute before adding them to the bath.

2. Add 5–10 drops of ylang ylang essential oil blended with a tablespoon of carrier oil to the bath water.

3. Lie back in the bath and allow the aroma of the ylang ylang oil and the energy of the agate stones to fill you with confidence.

CITRINE CRYSTAL BATH FOR A FRESH START

To embark on a different phase in your life, turn to the powerful combination of citrine crystals for new beginnings with orange essential oil to lift your mood.

YOU WILL NEED

Small bag of tumble polished citrine crystals, good-quality pure orange essential oil, carrier oil of choice (such as fractionated coconut oil, sweet almond oil, or jojoba oil), bath filled with water at a temperature you prefer

1. Cleanse the citrine crystals under water for a minute before adding them to the bath.

2. Add 5–10 drops of orange essential oil blended with a tablespoon of carrier oil to the bath water.

3. Lie back in the bath to enjoy the aroma of the orange oil and feel the power of the citrine crystals as they give you the strength to start anew.

CASE STUDY: Amanda's Story

My client Amanda had problems sleeping for about eight weeks before she came to see me. She was upset after losing her very stressful job, had constant headaches, was exhausted, and spent her whole time worrying about her finances and what she was going to do.

Worrying can bring on more worry and trigger a cycle of emotions that become more intense as you feel anxious, afraid, overwhelmed, and become unable to focus on anything. When you send out negative thoughts to the universe, they'll keep coming back to you at double and triple their intensity until you STOP!

I introduced Amanda to amethyst to help with her anxiety and headaches and suggested she try putting amethyst crystals in her bath every evening with some lavender essential oil and a carrier oil (see Amanda's Amethyst Crystal and Lavender Oil Recipe, opposite). I also suggested that she sleep with a lavender pillow and an amethyst crystal underneath it.

The combination of amethyst crystals and lavender essential oil is very powerful and effective. Amanda immediately felt the benefits and began to relax. Her headaches eased and she was able to sleep after her first bath. Once she began to relax and started looking at her life in a more constructive way, she felt more confident and happier in herself. She realized that she needed to look for a different type of job that was more suited to her personality and needs. Four weeks later she found her dream job. Amanda loved the benefits she received from her crystals and essential oils, and she has learned about other combinations and their benefits. She has continued to have a bath every evening and highly recommends them, especially to help with muscle aches and pains after a workout at the gym.

AMANDA'S AMETHYST CRYSTAL AND LAVENDER OIL RECIPE

When you are feeling stressed and anxious, or perhaps finding it challenging to sleep, try taking a bath every evening with amethyst crystals and lavender essential oil to benefit from their soothing and calming properties.

YOU WILL NEED

Small bag of tumble polished amethyst stones, good-quality pure lavender essential oil, carrier oil of choice (such as fractionated coconut oil, sweet almond oil, or jojoba oil), bath filled with water at a temperature you prefer

1. Cleanse the amethyst stones under water for a minute before adding them to the bath.

2. Add 5–10 drops of lavender essential oil blended with a tablespoon of carrier oil to the bath water.

3. Lie back in the bath to enjoy the calming effects of the amethyst crystals and lavender oil.

If you don't want to have a bath and prefer to take a shower, you can still benefit from using crystals and essential oils. Indulge yourself with an aromatherapy diffuser and choose your essential oil. You only need a couple of tiny drops of essential oil to give you a lovely aroma.

Use the essential oils I have mentioned in this book or choose a different one that complements how you are feeling. Surround your diffuser with a circle of crystals to give you healing energy and good vibrations. Scented candles can also be relaxing or uplifting, depending on the fragrance you choose, and can add to the mood, especially after a long day at work or looking after little ones!

Elixirs for Your Well-Being

Everything you do to take care of yourself will contribute to boosting your health and well-being and help you get to a better place to manifest your dreams. You can use crystals in elixirs and potions, as well as for crystal baths. Here are a couple of ideas for how to use them in this way.

ROSE QUARTZ ELIXIR

Another lovely way to benefit from rose quartz and other crystals is to use them in a homemade elixir. Elixirs are made from water energized with crystal energy. Note that some crystals are dangerous and best avoided. These include malachite, which can leach copper, and bumble bee jasper, which contains arsenic. The crystals in this book are all safe to use in an elixir apart from malachite. If you

LOVE POTION

This amazing love potion does exactly what it says: it gives you love! It's a combination of various aromatherapy oils, which can be used as bath oils, body oils for massage, facial and body creams, and so much more. You can choose the fragrance that will benefit you for a particular ailment such as aches and pains or for giving yourself love. Try dabbing behind the ears.

YOU WILL NEED

1 ml essential oil pipette dropper.

Glass roller bottle.

Good-quality pure essential oils—if you're not sure what to use, consult a professional aromatherapist, or use the following blend:

5 drops of rose essential oil, for love.

3 drops of neroli essential oil, for relieving stress.

2 drops of clary sage essential oil, for soothing, calming, and balancing.

2 drops of sandalwood essential oil, for promoting mental and physical health.

Three-quarters coconut oil as the carrier oil.

Moonstone, rose quartz, and garnet chips for goddess and god empowerment, love, and manifestation.

Note: If you would prefer to use more drops of a particular essential oil, then adjust accordingly. Everyone's sense of smell is different, but be careful not to overdo it. Essential oils can also have contraindications, so check with your local aromatherapist. Ideally, use vegan-friendly essential oils.

would like to use other crystals, please check their suitability from a reputable guide (see Philip Permutt, *The Crystal Healer*, 2 vols, CICO Books, 2016 and 2018).

To make a rose quartz elixir, leave a few tumble polished rose quartz crystals in a pitcher of water or water bottle in your fridge overnight. Then drink the elixir during the day, adding it to a water bottle if necessary for when you are away from home. This elixir always tastes sweet to me and gives me a sense of comfort and loving vibes. I've specifically chosen rose quartz here as a focal point for giving yourself love. When you let go of what doesn't serve you and give yourself love, this opens your heart, mind, body, and spirit to the magic of manifesting your dreams!

"The best is yet to come."

William Shakespeare

Only apply love potion in the glass roller bottle. Fill the glass roller bottle. Start by adding the moonstone, rose quartz, and garnet chips first to your glass roller bottle. Then:

- Add ¾ of the fractionated coconut carrier oil.

- Now add the essential oils individually using the pipette.

- 5 drops of rose essential oil, for love.

- 3 drops of neroli essential oil, for relieving stress and is uplifting.

- 2 drops of clary sage essential oil, for soothing, calming, and balancing.

- 2 drops of sandalwood essential oil, for promoting mental and physical health.

Then apply the love potion as needed to specific points such as the back of the wrists, behind the ears, or on the neck with your glass roller bottle. Remember, you must always dilute essential oils with a carrier oil if you are applying them directly to the skin, giving a massage, or dabbing them on specific points.

All essential oils need to be diluted with a carrier oil such as fractionated coconut oil, sweet almond oil, almond oil, or jojoba oil. Carrier oils are natural and add density to the essential oils, making them much smoother and gentler on the body. Without carrier oils, essentials oils would be too strong to apply to the body or use in creams and lotions.

Chakras and Essential Oils

Using essential oils that connect with your chakras can help to rebalance chakras that are out of alignment. If you feel that one of your chakras needs some extra love and attention, you can do this with essential oils too. When I'm working with private clients or a group of students, I'll often give them a couple of drops of rose oil blend to massage into their Heart chakra, the back of the wrists, and behind the ears. This promotes a sense of calm and well-being.

Here are some essential oils that can help to rebalance your chakras and give you the boost you need. Blend them with a carrier oil, such as fractionated coconut oil, almond oil, jojoba oil, or another oil of your choice, and massage gently into the chakra you are working on. Below I have suggested an essential oil that resonates with each of the seven chakras to enhance your well-being.

CHAKRA	ESSENTIAL OIL	CONNECTION
Crown	Frankincense	For spiritual connection
Brow	Lemon	For planning and new ideas and dreams
Throat	Peppermint	For communication
Heart	Rose	For giving yourself love
Solar plexus	Grapefruit	For confidence and courage
Sacral	Ylang ylang	For creativity and stimulating sexual energy
Base	Patchouli	For connection to the Earth and moving forward

Finding Your Inner God or Goddess

When you give yourself the care and self-love you need and cleanse yourself of what no longer serves you by letting go and making positive changes, your inner god or goddess will begin to shine through. Your inner goddess is your divine feminine energy; she is kind and loving, and she surrounds herself with other powerful energy. Your inner god is your divine masculine energy; he is passionate and gives you the strength to achieve and surrounds himself with power, energy, and courage.

The Moon is feminine energy that is very empowering. The Sun is your masculine inner god for divine male energy. We all have our inner god and goddess, whatever gender we are.

For female energy, moonstone is the crystal to hold and keep with you.

For masculine energy, sunstone is the crystal to embrace.

Who and What Makes You Smile?

Remembering who and what makes you happy can motivate you to start feeling good again. Think about friends and loved ones who make you happy. Remember the times you have smiled because of something as simple as feeling the warmth of the sun on your face.

EXERCISE: **Tell Your Stars**

1. Do this exercise by writing inside the stars, but first photocopy this page to create extra stars in case you would like to add more thoughts or ideas later.

2. Write down different things in each star that make you feel happy and smile. It may be a person or a situation. Fill the stars with feel-good moments.

3. Take a photo of what you have written and look at it daily to remind yourself of what makes you smile and feel happy.

IN SUMMARY: Tips to Remember

1. Give yourself some love with a daily hand cream meditation.

2. Give yourself a weekly self-healing treatment with your Circle of Self-Care chakra crystals.

3. Embrace what you love about yourself.

4. Remind yourself of what you can and have achieved.

5. Look at your stars—they'll remind you what makes you smile.

6. Remember to take time for yourself using your self-care wheel.

7. Give yourself a crystal treatment.

8. Relax in a crystal and essential oil bath.

YOUR GUIDE TO SHOWING YOURSELF LOVE

Let go of what doesn't serve you and give yourself love.

Open your heart to receiving new opportunities.

Value yourself.

Embrace new positive energy.

chapter 3

Let's Start Manifesting

Manifesting is an exciting and powerful process that helps you receive what you really want by focusing your intent on it and making it happen!

There are different ways to help you manifest and send out positive messages to the universe that you are ready to receive, as you release all that doesn't serve you. You will then be able to clear your mind, body, and spirit of any blockages and become open to the many wonderful possibilities of manifesting. If you procrastinate and aren't sure what you want, the universe will keep giving you things you're not sure of. Once you know what you are wishing for, stay focused on it.

It's important to focus on one thing at a time. Maybe it's happiness, abundance, love and romance, or a new job. Or perhaps there are other areas in your life that you crave to change. This may take time as you slowly work through this beautiful process of releasing, renewing, and receiving.

Believing in yourself, trusting in the process, and releasing negative thoughts, feelings, and memories that don't serve you will give you so much more peace, calm, and confidence.

Once you are in this place of openness, belief, and trust you are ready to Manifest Your Everything.

How Grateful Are You?

Being grateful for the air that you breathe, the sky that is blue, and the sun that shines are things that many people take for granted. As you go about your everyday life you may have forgotten how grateful you are to wake up every morning with a roof over your head and food to eat. Maybe you've been too busy complaining and moaning about life and everyone in it!

When was the last time you told yourself how grateful you are for who is and who was in your life, and how much you appreciated them? Did you tell them? Life can become full of complaints and non-stop moaning about what you haven't got when we should be grateful for what we do have instead. Rushing from one place to another and moaning about your schedule from the moment your alarm goes off in the morning until you go to bed at night can be exhausting. **Stop! Slow down! Smile and be grateful for what you do have.**

Being ungrateful and moaning about what you do have is a constant reminder to the universe that you only want what you've got. If you keep sending out ungrateful signals, you'll continue to get more of what you don't want.

FEELING GRATEFUL FOR WHAT YOU HAVE

Thinking about what you are truly grateful for can open up all kinds of possibilities for you to receive what you are manifesting. It also gives you a sense of peace, calm, and hope.

EXERCISE: WHO AND WHAT ARE YOU GRATEFUL FOR IN LIFE?

In the spaces below, note down five things in your life that you are grateful for:

I am grateful for ....

I am grateful for ....

I am grateful for ....

I am grateful for ....

I am grateful for ....

"Be thankful for what you have;
you'll end up having more.
If you concentrate on what you
don't have, you will never, ever
have enough."

Oprah Winfrey

The Power of Prayer and Being Grateful

The power of prayer sends so much good will, kind-heartedness, and compassion to yourself and others. Prayer is a wonderful spiritual practice that can be interpreted in many ways regardless of your belief system. It works with every tradition, belief, faith, and religion.

If you focus your intent in a positive way, the benefits of prayer can improve your mental and physical self. Prayer, like meditation, can help you become more self-aware and influence your state of mind and how you feel when you know in your heart what you want and who you are. Loving yourself unconditionally, feeling grateful for what you have, and being confident about who you are will help you expand the different experiences and positive results you have with prayer and meditation.

Love yourself unconditionally.

Feel grateful for what you have.

Feel confident about who you are.

In every spiritual tradition there is some sort of connection with the divine, whether that divinity is inside or outside yourself. If it is "inside the self," it is your divine god and goddess empowerment (see Finding Your Inner God or Goddess, page 57). If it's "outside the self," it could be the god of Judaism, Christianity, or Islam, or the forces of nature, perhaps in the form of trees (see Remarkable Trees, page 24) or a full moon. Maybe it's asking spirit to help you or just a feeling you get that gives you inner peace and calm. Other mystical traditions that focus on the "inside of the self" include Kabbalism, Sufism, and Gnosticism, as well as Eastern traditions like Buddhism and Hinduism which focus on meditation instead of prayer.

Whatever your spiritual tradition and focus, you can benefit from the following spiritual prayer:

Gratitude Meditation Prayer

Thank you for the birds and the bees, the Sun, Moon, and stars,

I'm so grateful to see nature thrive and be alive to breathe in fresh air every day.

Thank you for people in my life that care,

I'm so grateful to you.

Thank you to friends and loved ones who have passed on to a place in the sky,

I miss you and I am so grateful to have known and loved you, and will carry your inspiration and beautiful light and love with me always.

Thank you for the food I eat and the home I live in.

I am so grateful,

I am so grateful to have a roof over my head when I know how much so many in the world are suffering.

Thank you for my beautiful family,

I appreciate you all so much.

I am so grateful to have you in my life,

Thank you for your positive influence.

I am so grateful.

Thank you for giving me life and the lessons you have taught me to enable me to grow.

I am so grateful and appreciate you.

Thank you xx

EXERCISE: Write Your Own Gratitude Meditation Prayer

Write your own gratitude meditation prayer that resonates with you. Think of things that you are thankful and grateful for. When you write down your own meditation prayer and say it out loud this can make you more aware of what and who you appreciate in your life. It can also give you more peace, calm, and love to yourself.

1. Think of what and who you are grateful for in life. Refer to the Who and What Are You Grateful For? exercise on page 62 where you wrote down five things you are grateful for. Add these to your gratitude meditation prayer, which can be as long or as short as you want.

2. Take a photograph of your prayer and print it out, then laminate it and put it on your wall (you might want to type and print it instead before laminating).

3. Save the prayer on your phone or keep a photograph of it with you, so you can look at it wherever you are.

4. Give the prayer to a friend or loved one who might also benefit from your thoughts.

5. Look at your prayer every day to remind you what you are grateful for.

Give Yourself a Hug of Love

Self-hugging may seem a little awkward at first, but if you're giving yourself love and self-care, then a hug will elevate your feelings of happiness and love for yourself. It gives you a release of endorphins to lift your mood and the chemical oxytocin, or the "love hormone," which gives you a lovely warm feeling. It also helps you to manage feelings such as empathy and trust.

Give yourself a hug right now!

Hugging others can also give you immense comfort and support and provide you with a sense of safety if you're feeling afraid or upset. I call hugging "the natural healer." It's as though you give a huge sigh of relief when someone hugs you and you hug them. You don't need words—just the action.

When was the last time you hugged a friend or family member? When you have an opportunity to give them a hug, just do it and feel the benefits of the lovely feeling of support and well-being that comes over you.

Being Grateful to Others

When you are grateful and appreciative of others, think how good it makes you feel. Yet being grateful not only has a positive effect on yourself, but also on those you say thank you to. It's a wonderful way to spread positivity and will help you become more focused and optimistic. It gives the person receiving your gratitude a feeling of self-worth and appreciation. Gratitude toward others can make them smile from within and give them a gift of happiness.

When was the last time you told a friend, loved one, or work colleague how grateful you are for the kindness they show and the positive influence they have on your life? It may be just what they needed to hear from you! It also gives you a sense of happiness and well-being as you realize what you already have in your life.

Tell someone how much you appreciate them and how grateful you are for all they do.

A few words can mean so much.

Thank you!

I appreciate you!

I am so grateful!

MY GRATITUDE JOURNAL

Keep a journal and write down everything you are grateful for in life. Read the journal regularly to remind yourself of what's in it.

Gratitude and Manifestation

When you acknowledge that you are grateful for all you have, and have had, this raises your vibrations and increases your positive focus when you begin to manifest.

CASE STUDY: Annie's Story

Annie dreamed of having her own beauty salon offering alternative therapies, including Reiki, crystal healing, and meditation, as well as beauty treatments such as facials and manicures. She was determined to make it happen!

At first, Annie blamed her health for preventing her from moving forward with her dream. She had fibromyalgia—a medical condition that causes chronic pain in different areas of the body. Fatigue, depression, and hypersensitivity are just a few of the symptoms that affected her.

Living with chronic pain and other conditions is very challenging and debilitating, but Annie wasn't going to give in to this. Her acceptance and positive attitude toward her condition has helped immensely. She focused on what she could do to make positive change in her life and manifest her dream.

Annie gave herself self-healing crystal and Reiki treatments in between seeing me and meditating every day, which had a wonderfully positive impact. She did the "Manifest Your Everything" journey with me and started to give herself the unconditional love and care she deserved. She focused on letting go of anything that didn't serve her, which included saying goodbye to the grief of the devastating loss of both her parents at an early age that she had refused to acknowledge and accept for ten years.

We talked about the good memories she had of her parents and younger sister. She hadn't looked at any photos or watched videos of them for ten years. Her parents had owned a beautiful home in Los Angeles where her sister still lived with their aunt. Annie found it too painful to go there and moved to New York. She came to London for a year and stayed with friends while she took various healing courses with me and my partner, and she began embracing life again.

> "Dare to live the life you have dreamed for yourself. Go forward and make your dreams come true."
>
> Ralph Waldo Emerson

Remembering the good times and changing her perspective made Annie smile. She felt relieved, as she was able to let go of the pain of losing her parents and remember the good times they had together as a family. Annie focused on what she was grateful for and what she had in her life. She appreciated all the support she had from incredible friends.

When Annie let go of the painful feelings of grief she had been holding onto for ten years, she cried on and off for almost a week. The relief she felt was immense. By focusing on what she was grateful for and appreciating the good times she'd had, she was able to take more control of her emotions and the pain from her health condition. It was so wonderful to see the results.

One of the first things Annie did was to book a flight to Los Angeles and face going home to be with her sister and aunt. It was a different feeling this time and she felt more peaceful and content within.

She was now ready to manifest her dream of a beauty salon offering alternative therapies and wanted her aunt and sister to be involved in it too, so she moved back home to Los Angeles permanently.

Two years later, Annie's dream came true! A store came up for rent near their home! It was perfect! With her family and friends' support and help she opened her alternative beauty therapy salon. She takes care of herself daily and manages her health condition. Annie knows when to work hard and when to stop and rest.

Annie is truly grateful for all she has in her life and says her own thank you prayer every day.

Reframing Negative Thoughts and Choosing Positive Ones

When you have been focusing on the negative for a long time, you need to train your brain to start thinking positively and so change the outcomes of your behavior toward both yourself and how you come across to others.

If you tell yourself "I'm never going to change" or "I'm stuck, and no one can help me," then you'll stay in this negative pattern. Reframing these thoughts can start to give you a new outlook on how you deal with your life and challenging situations (see Affirmations, page 90).

The negative thoughts you have don't serve you. These negative beliefs can change your mood, so you may think you are not worthy of love and meeting your perfect partner, for example, or will never be able to do the job you have always dreamed of because you aren't good enough.

Reframing involves looking at your negative beliefs in a different way, from a positive perspective, and changing the words around to give a positive focus to what you are telling yourself. The more you practice reframing your thoughts, the more you can change your mindset to a positive one and start feeling happier and relieved from not constantly focusing on what hasn't helped you mentally or physically.

EXERCISE PART 1: Identify and Reframe Your Beliefs

Write down ten negative beliefs you are constantly saying to yourself and others in the table opposite—the first three have been done for you here. Then reframe these beliefs to positive ones in the spaces provided.

NEGATIVE THOUGHT	POSITIVE THOUGHTS REFRAME
"I'm never going to change my mindset"	"I'm going to change my mindset
"I'm stuck and no one can help me"	"I am open to getting help"
"No one's ever going to want to be with me"	"I will meet someone who loves me"

EXERCISE PART 2: **Identify and Reframe Your Thoughts**

Now write down ten negative thoughts you have and reframe them to positive ones in the spaces provided.

NEGATIVE THOUGHTS

1. ....
2. ....
3. ....
4. ....
5. ....
6. ....
7. ....
8. ....
9. ....
10. ....

POSITIVE THOUGHTS REFRAME

1. ....
2. ....
3. ....
4. ....
5. ....
6. ....
7. ....
8. ....
9. ....
10. ....

EXERCISE PART 3: **Dealing with Negative Thoughts**

It is your choice to choose how you think, what you say to yourself, and how you project yourself to others (see Chapter 4, page 84).

1. Every time a negative thought comes into your mind, shout out loud—or say to yourself if you're with other people—**STOP!**

2. Count backward from 10.

3. Anchor a moment that made you feel good for 30 seconds. (See Anchoring, page 76, and examples below to anchor positive, happy, memories.)

4. Think of the negative thought again and repeat steps 1 to 3 five times.

5. This exercise this will help you to **train your brain to focus on the positive** every time a negative thought comes into your head. The more you practice it, the easier it will become.

Crystal Manifestation: Amazing Stones of Transformation

This next part of your journey introduces you to the powerful energy of manifestation crystals.

Choosing the right crystal to manifest with will bring about a positive change. Each type of crystal can help you focus on different aspects of your life, so it's important to find the right crystal to work with. The powerful energy of crystals will help you to manifest what you are wishing for.

Choose a crystal from the list opposite that focuses and resonates with what you need. These are three of my favorite crystals to work with. I find them amazingly powerful to help manifest my dreams.

Manifestation Quartz: This is any quartz crystal that has another quartz crystal growing either straight up the middle inside or any other crystal such as fluorite or pyrite completely enclosed within it.

Brandberg Amethyst: This crystal is wonderful for helping you manifest inner peace, creativity, abundance, and love and romance. It can only be found at the Brandberg, which is Namibia's highest mountain, and is a combination of smoky quartz, amethyst, and clear quartz.

Mad Manifestation Crystal from Madagascar: This specific type of quartz crystal, which exhibits a clearly defined white quartz crystal growing within it, is found in Madagascar. It is wonderfully helpful for manifestating any of your dreams.

These are just a few of the incredible quartz crystals known for manifestation.

CHOOSING A CRYSTAL: WHAT DO I WANT TO MANIFEST?

Every crystal that is connected to what you want will manifest your wish with its amazing flow of unique, positive, and vibrant energy. There are suggestions for crystals to use for the different areas you may wish to manifest in the table below:

ROSE QUARTZ
Love and romance

CARNELIAN
Happiness

MALACHITE
Sleep

RHODOCHROSITE
Passion

GREEN CALCITE
Calm

TIGER'S EYE
Courage

CHRYSOCOLLA
New relationships

AMETHYST
Spirituality

GREEN AVENTURINE
Success

CRAZY LACE AGATE
Confidence

RAINBOW FLUORITE
Creativity

KYANITE
Communication

GARNET
Energy

RAINBOW MOONSTONE
Fertility

QUARTZ CRYSTAL
Health

CITRINE
Abundance

HERKIMER DIAMOND
New beginnings

TOURMALINE
Protection

MORGANITE
Self-love

SAPPHIRE
Achieving goals

ORANGE CALCITE
Smiling

JADE
Peacefulness

EXERCISE: **Your Manifestation Crystal Meditation**

1. Think about what you want to manifest and focus on that for every step of this manifestation crystal meditation.

2. Choose a manifestation crystal that resonates with what you want to manifest in this meditation (see page 73).

3. Hold the crystal in your left hand to receive from the universe.

4. Sit in an upright position on a chair, sofa, or bed with the palms of your hands facing up and resting on your thighs.

5. Close your eyes or focus on one area of the room such as a corner or area of the floor. Or look outside a window, perhaps at the leaves on a tree or the grass in the garden.

6. Relax your neck and shoulders and imagine a piece of string from the top of your head gently pulling you up to the sky so your spine is nice and straight.

7. Take a slow, deep breath in through your nose for a count of 4 and then slowly release through your mouth for a count of 5. Repeat this three times.

8. Now find a comfortable breath pattern for you and breathe normally.

9. Feel the crystal in your hand. Is there a tingling sensation? Does it feel warm or cold?

10. Now imagine the crystal in your hand getting bigger and bigger until you're looking up at it!

11. See the crystal sparkling in front of you and notice a beautiful ray of colored light shining from the inside. This might be a reflection of the color of the crystal, such as a purple color if you're holding an amethyst, or a golden

light if you're holding citrine. There may be an entrancing rainbow color flowing out toward you or a combination of any colors that work for you.

12. As the light flows out of the crystal, feel the warmth of the glow as it surrounds you.

13. Now imagine an open arch at the front of your crystal and step into its encapsulating light of manifestation.

14. Whatever you want to manifest, as you step inside your crystal imagine that it is happening right now. Believe it, feel it, and embrace this moment. This is what you want! Experience how it feels and hear the wonderful sounds around you! Maybe there is a specific job you're passionate about and have always dreamed of—see yourself doing it and loving every moment. The feeling is real and so powerful. Perhaps you imagine that you are in a kind, loving, and beautiful relationship where you can see and hear yourself smiling, laughing, and feeling so happy. Focus on what you want in your light of manifestation.

15. Stay in the moment for 5–10 minutes, or longer if you wish. Enjoy every moment.

16. Breathe in the light while you are "inside" the crystal. Feel and see it fill your mind, body, and spirit with hope, energy, and a wonderful connection to the life you want to create.

17. Hold onto these feelings as you step out of the crystal and stand looking at the beautiful rays of light flowing from it.

18. Now imagine the crystal becoming smaller and smaller until you can feel it in the palm of your hand once more.

19. Take a slow, deep breath in through your nose and slowly out through your mouth three times.

20. Open your eyes and take a few minutes to embrace how you are feeling.

Anchoring

Anchoring is a way of connecting a positive memory with a physical action such as squeezing your thumb and forefinger together. This enables you to bring the energy of the memory into the present moment to help you feel good. You can anchor a memory to feel anything, from confident and positive to calm and relaxed. Different triggers may remind you of something good—perhaps a song that brings back a memory of fun times you had with friends or a hot bright sun that evokes a memory of feeling relaxed and calm lying on a beach.

EXERCISE: Anchor a Special Memory

Use this simple exercise to anchor a positive memory in your mind. You can anchor different memories that relate to your emotions at the time.

1. Remember a time that made you feel good.

2. Take a slow, deep breath in through your nose and then breathe out slowly through your mouth as your shoulders relax and you start to breathe normally.

3. Imagine being in the moment you want to remember. Maybe you see yourself having a relaxing massage or laughing with family or friends during a fun evening out.

4. Squeeze your thumb and forefinger together and stay focused in this place of feeling good.

5. Now double and triple the good feelings. Make them bigger, brighter, and bolder and turn up the volume to hear yourself laughing and having fun! Double and triple these feelings again to heighten them even more!

6. Feel yourself smile as you enjoy being back in this memory! Stay in this wonderful place of feeling good for 5 minutes.

> **"Imagination is everything. It is the preview of life's coming attractions."**
>
> Albert Einstein

7. Take a slow, deep breath in through your nose and then slowly breathe out through your mouth.

8. Open your eyes and release your thumb and forefinger.

9. Now you can revisit this memory and enjoy its benefits whenever you want to. Just squeeze your thumb and forefinger together and this action will take you straight there!

10. You can also use this technique to create other things, whether you need a boost of confidence or something to make you laugh or relax.

HOW TO ANCHOR A SPECIAL MEMORY

Thinking about a memory, and noting down how it makes you feel, can help you anchor it in you mind and recall it more easily:

Write down your memory:

....

....

How does your memory make you feel? Write down three things:

1. ....

2. ....

3. ....

See Your Dreams Come to Life

This exercise is another powerful way to bring your dreams to life through positive visualization. It gives you the power to acknowledge what you want and how you want it to look—as part of the Manifest Your Everything process.

Imagine you are the producer and director of your own movie. See the movie become real as you visualize what you want to manifest. It's your choice to decide how you run this movie in your mind. If you don't like something, you can rewrite the script and change the scenes, just as you have choices to change a situation that doesn't serve you in real life. When you send your wishes to the universe with positive intent and focus, it will send you back what you ask for.

EXERCISE: Turn Your Dream into Reality

1. Close your eyes. Focus on what you are dreaming of and see this as if it's on a movie screen in front of you.

2. Step into your movie as you see, feel, and hear everything around you.

3. Make your movie a Hollywood blockbuster and see the queues around the block waiting to watch it. Hear your name called out at the Oscars and all the applause! See your name in lights!

4. Now see the movie become your reality and part of the life you are wishing for.

5. Change the queues around the block into anything your want! Maybe it's friends or family praising you for your achievements or the Oscar you receive becomes a person and the love of your life you've been waiting for.

6. As the movie in your mind becomes clearer and clearer, feel how good it is to have what you wish for.

7. Thank the universe for sending you the life you're dreaming of as if you already have it.

8. Open your eyes and come back into the room. Your movie will keep rolling. Stay focused on it and what you want. The movie will become reality when you're ready to receive it.

Summoning Inspiration

Inspiration can give you the enthusiasm and positive boost for your creativity to flow and encourage you to do something you've always wanted to. Being inspired by someone can help you feel motivated enough to take action and follow your passion, whether this is traveling the world or training to run a marathon for a charity of your choice. Anyone can be your inspiration, from a movie star to a family friend or colleague.

Answer the following questions to help you focus more clearly on finding your inspiration:

Who inspires you?

What does this person do to inspire you?

How have they inspired you?

FINDING A ROLE MODEL

I have always been a huge fan of Whoopi Goldberg! She inspires me with her vivacious personality, tenacity, and impactful screen presence. Being inspired by someone can enable you to focus on the area you want to bring out in yourself. Focusing on the inspiration you get from them can also encourage you to feel what you want to feel.

Always remember you are unique and the person who inspires you is unique too. The qualities you see in them, such as confidence and strength, are already inside you too and just need an extra boost to resurface again.

Remember, inspiration can come from many other sources, including from art or from nature, (see The Inspirational Power of Nature case study overleaf.)

CASE STUDY: Movie Star Hero (Tyler's Story)

When working with a national league sports team I asked who inspired them.

Tyler stood up! Everyone looked round and cheered him! He was brilliant at scoring on the field and usually never joined in any discussions at a workshop unless specifically asked! Tyler said he was inspired by my topic of manifesting what you want. He explained that he always visualized scoring and winning! He admired and was inspired by Arnold Schwarzenegger in the movie *Terminator 2*—he thought he was strong, heroic, and sincere.

Arnie's character was Tyler's inspiration as he ran through the tunnel with the crowds cheering and out onto the field, ready to score several times for his team and fans! He always succeeded and made everyone very happy!

CASE STUDY: The Inspirational Power of Nature (Jan's Story)

Jan needed inspiration for decorating her apartment and bringing color and a feeling of warmth back into her home. She was also looking for love and to manifest romance. But she wanted to focus on taking care of herself and her needs first before meeting the right partner. Every time she went to an interior design store or asked friends for advice, she wasn't inspired by anything.

Jan decided to spend some time in the mountains during the fall and explore nature and its breathtaking colors. She was excited to do something for herself and had the most wonderful experience discovering what she loved. This made her feel happy and proud of herself for doing what she wanted. The richness of the reds, yellows, oranges, and greens set against a stunning blue sky gave her all the inspiration she needed. She collected different samples of colored leaves that had fallen to the ground and took lot of photos, which she stuck in a large notebook called "My Home Inspiration." Doing something inspirational, like Jan, can lead you to discover so many other areas in your life that you didn't even realize were missing.

Jan loved her newly decorated home inspired by nature and all the colors of the fall, and she was now ready to manifest a love interest into her life. She didn't realize how much she had been putting up an obvious block to meeting anyone until she felt ready. Jan's best friend and work colleague had waited patiently and not mentioned how she felt until she knew that Jan was more open to having a relationship. Jan was so surprised when she found out because she'd had no idea that the love of her life was right in front of her all the time!

When you release any blocks that have been holding you back and let down your barriers of resistance, you can suddenly see things or people in a different light and open your heart to so many possibilities.

A Smile Can Say More Than a Thousand Words

Come rain or shine, if you put a smile on your face, it changes how you feel from the inside out. A smile also radiates love, warmth, and happiness to others, is a wonderful stress-reliever, and helps boost your mood. Even when you give a false smile there's something inside you that's saying "Come on, you can do this." So, let go of these negative, stressful feelings and just SMILE!

Smiling releases endorphins in the same way that happens when you work out at the gym or go for a fast walk in nature. You still use your muscles to smile and there are lots of other benefits too, including reducing overall blood pressure and helping with pain. Smiling helps you feel so much better about you.

When was the last time you smiled at someone, and they smiled back? How did that make you feel? If you've been used to frowning, it is time for a change! Smile at yourself in the mirror! It may seem strange at first, but the more you do it, the more it will happen naturally. Waking up with a smile on your face can set you up for the day. Going to sleep with a smile on your face can help toward a peaceful night, sending out happy and positive messages to the universe.

I always think of the song "When You're Smiling (The Whole World Smiles With You!)," which was written in 1928. You can't help but sing along and have a big smile on your face every time you hear it! It's been sung by so many well-known artists, including Louis Armstrong, Frank Sinatra, and Michael Bublé.

Think of a "happy" moment you have anchored that makes you feel good and just smile! Every thought, every feeling you have goes straight to the universe and if it sees you smile, it will send you so much more to smile about!

IN SUMMARY: Tips to Remember

Everything you do, from self-hugging to feeling grateful, working with crystals to smiling can contribute to your mental and physical well-being and make a huge contribution to the powerful impact of manifesting your everything.

1. Embrace what you are truly grateful for and it will give you peace and open your heart to receiving what you want.

2. Call on the power of prayer to send so much good will, kind-heartedness, and compassion to yourself and others.

3. Use manifestation crystals—choosing the right crystal for you, depending on what you hope to manifest, will bring about positive change.

4. Anchor a moment that makes you feel good.

5. Bring your dreams to life through positive visualization. Imagine you are the producer and director of your own movie.

6. Be inspired by someone, as this can help you focus on the area you want to bring out in yourself.

7. Smile, as this can change how you look and feel from the inside out.

YOUR GUIDE TO MANIFESTING

Meditate to clear your mind and feel peaceful.

Accept and acknowledge what has been, as this will enable you to move forward, and how grateful you are.

Nurture and nourish your soul by embracing nature and give yourself what you need—use "me time" to indulge yourself with beautiful essential oils.

Be inspired and imagine what you want—let your intuition guide you.

Forgive and let that forgiveness free you from hurt and being the victim. Take back control and focus on what you are dreaming of (see Forgiveness, page 20).

Energize: rejuvenate and reawaken the energy you once had. Release blockages and embrace new beginnings.

Success: see yourself succeed in all you do and believe in yourself. Send your positive messages to the universe and the universe will hear you.

Trust: learn to trust yourself and what you want.

chapter 4

Your Messages to the Universe

Dreaming of living on a desert island, meeting your perfect partner, or getting your ideal job is possible! The good news is that anything can become reality if you focus on it, believe it will happen, and send your message to the universe. It may not happen in the next day, month, year, or longer; it will happen if you believe and it is right for you. Be patient, trust the universe has heard you, and never give up hope.

If the universe senses you're not sure and your vision isn't right for you, your dream won't happen. I'm a huge believer in receiving what is meant to be when the time is right. It's important to know in your heart what you really want.

There are many ways to manifest what you are wishing for. Through my own experiences and the work I do as a therapist and healer, I have spent many years developing the "Manifest Your Everything" journey. It's magical and empowering! It helps you create the life you want. By focusing, believing, and trusting in the process, you can experience an incredible, positive shift that helps you manifest your everything.

"If you can dream it, you can do it."

Walt Disney

Manifestation Vision Boards

Making your own manifestation vision board is one of the most powerful and impactful positive things you can do. By sticking words and images on a large board that represent the things you want to achieve, you can visualize what you want and focus on it every day. Your unconscious mind will then concentrate on positive outcomes.

Cut out pictures of your dream home, your perfect vacation, pet, or car! You may want to include pictures that represent finding love such as hearts and happy couples together. Or perhaps you have family and friends or work colleagues you want to include in your future vision. You can stick anything you want on your manifestation board. Words are just as powerful as pictures to illustrate what you are hoping for. So, also include notes such as "Having fun with my family on a holiday," "Opening up my life to be more spiritual," "Finding peace, calm, and happiness," "Having good health," "Being financially secure," and "Finding my dream job."

EXERCISE: **How to Make Your Manifestation Vision Board**

It is easy to create your own manifestation vision board. You will need some magazines, pictures, and photos, a computer and printer, a pair of scissors, some sticky tack or glue, and a piece of Ainsi-D (A1) white cardstock or a large pinboard.

1. Cut out the pictures that inspire you and see yourself with what you've chosen to put on your manifestation board. Include photos of places you have imagined going to or pictures of objects you'd like to have around you. Whatever you want, stick it on your board!

2. Wake up looking at your board and go to sleep at night looking at it. Take a photo of your board and look at it on your cellphone during the day. The more you focus on your board, the more you can imagine stepping into that moment and being there—however long it takes. See your dreams, feel them, hear them, and step into them as you imagine them becoming reality.

3. When one or more of your visions become reality, add other things you would like to your board.

4. When you come from a positive place and ask for what you wish for, the universe will hear you.

CASE STUDY: Lara's Story

One of my clients, Lara, had a vision of running a retreat on a Greek island. It was a huge challenge financially. I suggested that she put pictures on a large manifestation board, including every detail of the retreat she imagined, and then hang this on a wall where she would see it every day. About six months later, Lara had a phone call from a friend who had gone to live in Greece. She had recently moved to a beautiful place by the beach that had accommodation for ten people. Lara's friend was a wonderful cook and she suggested that between the two of them they could organize a well-being retreat.

Lara flew to Greece that month and loved it so much she stayed there! The retreat was exactly what she had visualized on her manifestation board. Every detail was there, from the bright, light therapy rooms to a large room downstairs—with pale oak wooden floors for yoga and stretch classes—overlooking the sea and a stunning, pale blue kitchen with matching tiles and whitewashed walls. It was her dream come true.

Lara had also manifested her perfect partner! He was her soul mate, best friend, and everything she'd always wanted in a relationship. He was kind, caring, and loving and they had so much in common, including a love of yoga, meditation, and a healthy lifestyle. She met him on her own retreat and he was everything she had put on her manifestation board.

Lara decided it was time to do a new manifestation board. Eight months later she got engaged to her man. She then planned the wedding of her dreams. They were married a year later and two years later had their first baby. They then moved to another beautiful island in Greece. Lara's vision of her new home still had whitewashed walls, a pale blue kitchen, and a room that overlooked the sea, to meditate in and do her daily yoga practice. Lara still dreams of having a retreat again, but her priorities have changed for a while. When she's ready, she'll start manifesting again.

As Lara's story shows, the more you focus on positive images, the more they can become reality, and your life can change for the better when you least expect it.

It's Your Choice

What you say to yourself can have a massive impact on how you feel and how the universe responds to your messages. Only you can decide what you think and what you tell yourself. If you choose negative words, they can become embedded in your unconscious mind as you continuously send messages to your brain that don't serve you well. The universe hears you and will keep sending you back what you're telling yourself. Changing your thought patterns to positive ones and telling yourself what you can do and achieve will create a shift in your subconscious and help you to focus more on positive outcomes. When you stop self-sabotaging and retrain your brain by breaking negative cycles, the universe will hear you and respond in a positive way by giving you what you want. See Reframing Negative Thoughts and Choosing Positive Ones, on page 70, for guidance on how to do this.

USING AFFIRMATIONS

Positive affirmations are a fabulous way of keeping yourself in the feel-good zone!

One of the ways to make sure the universe hears you every day is to say your affirmations out loud or quietly to yourself, depending on where you are. You can keep photos of them on your phone, or stick them on the fridge door or anywhere in your home that you'll see them. They're wonderful motivators and can inspire you to keep going and say "I can do this!"

"Nurture your mind with great thoughts, for you will never go any higher than you think."

Benjamin Disraeli

The more you use positive affirmations, the more they will become embedded in your unconscious mind and any negative words you use will shrink and become tiny specs of dust that just disintegrate. Here are some positive affirmations that may resonate with you:

Look in the mirror every day and tell yourself: "I love you." The more you do this, the more you will start to believe it and the more the universe will hear you and keep sending you loving energy!

I also suggest you do the word meditation (see Exercise 1: How to Meditate, page 22) and silently repeat the affirmations that resonate with you over and over until you are in a deep state of relaxation—for example, "I'm grateful for all I have, I feel proud, I feel happy and grounded." These words will become embedded in your unconscious mind. The more you meditate with them, the more they will surprise you and come into your conscious mind when you need a boost! Keep practicing!

I feel strength from within

i'm proud of myself

i have courage

I feel focused

i'm taking care of me

I feel grounded

I can, I will, and I want to!

Manifest Your Everything Ceremony

Now you have released what doesn't serve you, it's time to embrace what you do want to manifest and create in your life. The three-part manifestation ceremony below is uplifting and motivating, and will give you a sense of well-being, happiness, and hope for the future.

To do a manifestation ceremony, you'll need some sheets of letter-size (A4) paper, a pencil, ruler, and pen, a pair of scissors, a small singing bowl and mallet, a bundle of sage and large feather, an abalone shell dish or other fireproof dish, a small jar (such as jam jar), some dried rose petals, and a small rose quartz crystal.

EXERCISE PART 1:

Write Down Everything Positive You Are Wishing For

The first part of the ceremony is an opportunity for you to consider and write down everything you want to manifest in your life.

1. Draw horizontal lines in pencil across the sheets of paper. Now draw vertical ones, so you have lots of sections to write in.

2. Write down everything positive you want to manifest in your life in the sections, such as happiness, financial security, or true love. Think about what you want, including your dreams and passions, and all that inspires you. If you're looking for your soul mate, put that down! What else do you want from a romantic partner? Perhaps kindness, love, passion, someone who loves animals or children and will love your family. Make sure to write down every detail of what you're wishing for. Add all your positive affirmations to the mix too (see page 90)!

3. Cut out each section and fold the papers a few times.

This part of the ceremony is intended to help you manifest your everything, but remember to include all the things you want! As an example of why this is important, I'll use Samantha's story. Samantha was looking for love and romance and wrote down everything except passion. A month later she met someone. Everything she had manifested came true. She was so happy. When I saw her a few weeks later, she said it was all wonderful and the only thing missing was the passion! Some help was needed. I gave her some rhodochrosite, the crystal for passion, and suggested putting it discreetly under her loved one's pillow and on the nightstand as well as in other areas. It worked! Samantha also did another manifestation ceremony and asked for a few more wishes, including passion. She added these to her affirmation jar.

EXERCISE PART 2:

Enhance Your Manifestation With a Singing Bowl

This next part of the ceremony is a special ritual that includes cleansing and raising the vibrations of your words and messages to the universe by using the powerful sound of your singing bowl. This part of the exercise involves burning sage, so please ensure you use a well-ventilated room or work outside.

1. Once you have folded up all your, dreams, wishes, and affirmations, put them in the singing bowl.

2. Light one end of the sage bundle and then blow out the flame. Hold the sage bundle in one hand over the shell or fireproof dish to catch the ashes and the feather in your other hand. Now cleanse all around yourself and over the singing bowl by directing the sage smoke with the feather. (To find out more about cleansing with sage, see The Smudging Ceremony, page 31.)

3. Now place the singing bowl in the palm of your non-dominant hand and gently strike the outside with the mallet using your dominant hand.

4. Each time you strike the bowl I suggest giving the sound time to resonate and disperse before striking it again. This will send positive vibrations to your written words and out to the universe.

EXERCISE PART 3:
Keep Affirmations and Positive Wishes in A Jar

The final part of your manifestation ceremony is to place your positive words and messages into a beautiful jar with a small rose quartz crystal and rose petals to infuse love into your messages. This will keep reminding you of the positive dreams you wish for. Keep it nearby, hold it when meditating, or focus on the jar as you meditate and see, feel, and hear the words and messages become your reality.

1. Place the folded pieces of paper in the jar with some dried rose petals and a small rose quartz crystal to send love, peace, and happiness to your beautiful messages.

2. Keep your affirmation jar by the side of your bed or on your desk at work, or wherever you'd like to see it to remind you of your dreams and everything that is possible.

3. Continue to say your positive affirmations daily and focus on your wishes. The universe will hear you.

When you feel it's time for another manifestation ceremony, remember to include your positive affirmations. If everything from your jar has become reality, then start again with a new one and give yourself an extra boost of magic!

"Keep your thoughts positive because your thoughts become your words. Keep your words positive because your words become your habits. Keep your habits positive because your habits become your values. Keep your values positive because your values become your destiny."

Gandhi

Manifestation Crystal Grids

Let crystals join you in your manifestation and help give you what you desire. Creating a crystal grid can help you focus your positive intent.

Once you have chosen what you want to manifest, you can make a manifestation crystal grid and fill it with your chosen crystal (see Choosing a Crystal: What Do I Want to Manifest?, page 73). I also love to add flowers to bring in the beauty of nature, and sometimes candles, around the outside of my grid.

HOW TO MAKE A MANIFESTATION CRYSTAL GRID

The process below is the same for every manifestation crystal grid you create, but you use different crystals to manifest different things. If you're looking for love and romance, for example, then you should use rose quartz to make your grid.

You'll need a rose quartz crystal point, a rose quartz sphere, or larger rose quartz, six smaller pieces of rose quartz, six clear quartz crystal points, flowers and rose petals (optional), a round or square tray to place your crystal grid on. You may also have an area in your home on a table in the corner of your living room or your bedroom that you would like to cover with a fabric and place your grid on.

1. Choose a rose quartz crystal point, a rose quartz sphere, or a larger rose quartz in the center of the grid as your focus.

2. Place six smaller pieces of rose quartz around the central crystal. If you have a crystal point in the center, put one piece of rose quartz in each of the six corners creating a hexagonal shape. If you have a rose quartz sphere or a larger rose quartz the six pieces of rose quartz you place around it will create a circle. Whatever you choose to use will give you the outcome for your manifestation grid.

3. Put six clear quartz crystal points so they are facing inward toward each of the six pieces of rose quartz.

4. Now place a piece of rose quartz at the other end of each clear quartz crystal point.

5. If you wish, you can fill the grid with flowers or rose petals, or both. You can also add candles around the outside. Remember never to leave lit candles unattended.

6. Once your crystal grid is finished, leave it until you have received what you wished for from the universe.

MUSIC TO MOTIVATE AND ENHANCE YOUR MOOD

Once you have finished a manifestation ceremony, it can be helpful to clear your mind and have some fun playing music you love to sing along to, dance to, or just listen to. Music is a wonderful healer and can make you feel happy and enhance your mood. It can also help you feel calm and relaxed and reduce stress and anxiety. If you feel like dancing to the music, that is great, as it is a wonderful confidence booster and stress-reliever and is good for improving your well-being.

Some of the greatest songs have inspired, motivated, and given hope to so many. When was the last time you danced, listened to, or sang along to your favorite tunes? Do the words resonate with you? Music is a powerful tool to consider having in your life regularly to lift your morale and inspire you to have fun! See A Smile Can Say More Than a Thousand Words, on page 82, for more on how smiling can enhance your life.

"What the mind of man can conceive and believe, the mind of man can achieve."

Napoleon Hill

What Do You Want To Manifest To Create Your Dream Life?

Everything you have focused on from the very first chapter until now has led to this moment: to enable you to manifest your dreams with positive intent. Once you love yourself, feel peaceful within, and can clarify exactly what you want in a manifestation ceremony, the magic will happen.

If you want to create positive change in your life and manifest your dreams, nothing will happen if you don't take action to make it happen! This next section contains checklists to help you keep focused and track how well you're doing.

YOUR WEEKLY CHECK-IN PLAN

Check in with yourself every morning. Photocopy the following check-in pages and answer the questions every day for seven days. At the end of seven days, you will notice a change in your answers if you have been doing what I suggest in the preceding chapters. You may need to revisit a chapter to ensure you're providing yourself with what you need. This might be giving yourself even more love or peeling off more layers to let go of other things you're now ready to say goodbye to. This is your journey. Choose what you do with focus and clarity.

Repeat your check-in days if you feel you need an extra seven days. Do this seven-day check-in once a month to remind you how far you've come or what you need to do to help yourself feel happy and manifest all you wish for.

Remember: taking care of yourself is always a work in progress. It is constant!

Have you woken up with a smile on your face today?

 Yes   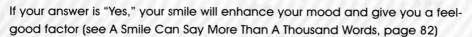 No

If your answer is "Yes," your smile will enhance your mood and give you a feel-good factor (see A Smile Can Say More Than A Thousand Words, page 82)

If your answer is "No," what are you going to do NOW to make a difference? Start smiling! Practice, Practice, Practice!

Do you feel energized?

 Yes   No

If your answer is "Yes," it sounds as if you are in a good place on your journey toward manifesting your everything. Keep focusing your positive intent to manifest your wishes and giving yourself the love you deserve.

If your answer is "No," there is some work to be done:

- What can you tell yourself? See Using Affirmations, on page 90. Are you getting enough sleep and looking after yourself physically? See Daily Routine for Positive Change, on page 122, for guidance on establishing a good daily routine.

- Are you giving yourself the self-care you need, including exercising regularly along with healthy eating? This can help enhance your mood and boost your energy levels (see page 126).

- Maybe you have more to let go of and need to revisit the burning ceremony (see Saying Goodbye with a Burning Ceremony, page 27) and give yourself more love (see Chapter 2 Giving Yourself Love).

THE ENERGIZING POWER OF GARNET

Garnet is a wonderful energizer. You can hold it at night, sleep with it under your pillow, or keep it next to you on your nightstand. Keep it with you all day. Once you begin to feel peace and happiness within, it is amazing how you can feel so much more energized and excited to get up, get out, and get going with your life!

What positive affirmations do you tell yourself every morning?

List 3 positive affirmations

1. ....

2. ....

3. ....

If you wake up focusing on the negatives, it's time to reframe your thoughts (see Reframing Negative Thoughts and Choosing Positive Ones, page 70). Start saying your positive affirmations NOW (see Using Affirmations, page 90)! Nothing will improve unless you change what you tell yourself. The release that you experience following your burning ceremony and cutting the cord can also have a huge impact on your mindset, giving you a feeling of relief, peace, freedom, and happiness (see the three-part exercise under Rituals for Letting Go, pages 26–28). Repeat this letting-go ceremony if you feel there is more you need to let go of. The more you do this, the more you will peel off the different layers that you need to say goodbye to.

How did you sleep?

In the star below, add your score from 1–10, with one being you hardly had any sleep and ten being you slept for a good seven or eight hours.

 Score

If your score is a low number, what can you do to help yourself sleep better? One suggestion is to have a relaxing crystal and essential oil bath before going to bed (see Amanda's Amethyst Crystal and Lavender Oil Recipe, page 53). You can also draw on the power of malachite, which is a wonderful crystal to help you sleep. Hold the malachite an hour before you go to bed, then either keep holding it or put it under your pillow or on your nightstand while you sleep. Do this every night for a week and write down your sleep score the following morning. Notice the difference in your scores from the first to last day. Always avoid cleansing malachite with water because it can leach copper. (See Cleansing Crystals, page 141.)

Have you done your morning meditation?

 Yes Ⅰ No

If your answer is "Yes" and you're meditating for a few minutes every morning, slowly start to increase your meditation time. If you are rushing in the morning, wake up 20 minutes earlier. The benefits are immense (see Release Inner Turmoil through Meditation, page 21).

If your answer is "No" and you aren't meditating every morning, then START NOW! Start with two minutes and build up to longer. Focus on the word meditation (see Exercise 1: How to Meditate, page 22), visualize a beautiful place you've been to, such as a spectacular waterfall surrounded by nature, or focus on dancing flames in your mind and see all the different colors brighten the light there. Whatever you meditate on, let everything else flow out of your mind and keep coming back to this focus.

I appreciate that for some people it is a challenge to meditate in the morning if you have a baby or toddler to look after. Perhaps you have a dog or cat that demands your attention too. Whatever it is, give yourself 2–5 minutes every morning when everyone is asleep to look after yourself. Meditating can give you a wonderful energy boost for the day and improve your mood. It may be just what you need first thing!

Meditating is also a wonderful practice to do in the early evening. It is relaxing and can take you into a lovely, comforting space to release any tension or stress from your day.

How much are you looking forward to your day?

In the star below, add your score from 1–10, with 1 being the lowest in terms of how much you're looking forward to your day and 10 being the highest because you can't wait!

 Score

If you've scored a 7 or under, what are you going to do to make positive changes NOW? Start focusing on reframing your thoughts (see Reframing Negative Thoughts and Choosing Positive Ones, page 70).

Manifesting your everything can be small things too! If it's important to you, then it is worth focusing on.

WRITE A LETTER TO YOURSELF

Imagine where you will be, what you will be doing, and who you will be with in a year's time. Think about what you want this person to be like and focus on the connection between you. Write down every detail you are wishing for in every situation you are looking to manifest.

How Do You Know You're Manifesting Correctly?

If you're noticing positive things happening, such as suddenly connecting with someone as they brush past you in the elevator at work or seeing photos of your dream home coming up on your phone, computer, and billboards, then things are starting to move in the right direction. Stay focused on what you are wishing for.

Sometimes when you're manifesting you might feel stuck and unsure of what you're asking for. When this happens, you may be sending the universe mixed messages, and it then receives the wrong signal from you and sends you what you don't want!

This may also be the universe telling you to start again because the path you are on is not right for you. Instead, you need to focus on a different path where you have clarity and positive intent and know exactly what you want without any doubts. What you wish for may not be what you really want!

Maybe you're still holding onto limiting beliefs such as "I will never meet the right person for me" or "I'm never going to find my dream house." Whatever is holding you back you need to LET GO!

Remember, this is your journey, and you can manifest anything, whether large or small. But be realistic! The timescale of asking for something very big could take months or years. It could also happen very quickly, depending on what it is. Start by focusing on things that might not take long to manifest and then if you're happy to wait, manifest the biggest goals you want to achieve. Be patient. Good things can take time, but they're worth waiting for!

START MANIFESTING SMALL THINGS FIRST

To gain confidence in the manifesting process, it is sensible to start small and build up from there. Below are two examples to get you started.

MANIFEST A TEXT OR PHONE MESSAGE

Ask to receive a text or phone message you've been hoping for. To do this, write down the name of the person you want to hear from and/or stick a photo of them on your manifestation vision board (see page 86). Feel grateful for what you have received and say thank you, even though you haven't heard from the person yet. When you haven't been in touch with someone for a long time and you begin to focus on them, magic can happen and you suddenly hear from them. When you put your positive intent out into the universe, it is amazing what comes back.

Let me give you an example of how this works. My very good friend Yvonne lives in Holland, and we can go for months without speaking! When we do, it only seems like yesterday that we last spoke! Something will happen—perhaps I'll eat in a restaurant that we love going to when we see each other, or her photo will randomly come up on my phone. Then I know that I need to call her. She'll always say that she was just thinking of me too and was going to call. Synchronicity is amazing. Does the universe hear you? Absolutely!

MANIFEST A PERFECTLY DELICIOUS DINNER

If you want to impress a loved one or are having a few friends round, and you want to make a delicious dinner they will remember, you can manifest that too. Firstly, show your chosen recipe and ingredients lots of love. Add photos to your manifestation vision board of your friends or loved ones smiling and laughing. Put photos of the ingredients and a picture of the recipe next to them. If there is a photo of the meal in your recipe book take a copy of it and add it to your manifestation board. The universe will see this as you visualize it becoming a wonderful reality! Write down the recipe and ingredients (see page 92), place them into your singing bowl (see page 93), and then into your positive wishes jar (see page 94). Use positive intent and focus before you begin to cook. Gather all the ingredients you need to make the meal, such as the vegetables and potatoes as well as meat, vegetarian, or vegan options. Then follow the recipe instructions carefully. Believe and trust that the meal is going to be fabulous—and it will be!

Once you have mastered manifesting a simple wish, you can start focusing your positive energy and intent on achieving bigger dreams and ambitions.

MANIFESTING BIGGER WISHES AND DREAMS

This section shows you how to manifest some of the bigger wishes and dreams people typically ask for, whether that is finding true love, buying a dream home, going on an amazing vacation, or being successful in life. The wishes and dreams described here all have a specific crystal I have chosen to enhance the power of what you are manifesting. There is a checklist of steps you can take that will help turn your dream into reality. Each one has its own unique steps for you to follow. Remember, each wish or dream will be unique to you, and will involve moving through different stages, so you can receive what you want.

Always go through the "Manifest Your Everything" process (summarized overleaf) before doing a manifestation ceremony for any of your wishes in all sections.

THE MANIFEST YOUR EVERYTHING PROCESS

Here is a reminder of the process you need to undergo to manifest your wishes successfully. This is crucial when you're working to achieve what you really want in your life such as finding love or buying the home of your dreams. Stages 1 to 10 should all be completed before performing a "Manifest Your Everything" ceremony. If you need help remembering how to do any of the following, then please refer to the relevant exercises in Chapters 1–4.

1. Let go and say goodbye to anything that no longer serves you
    (see Chapter 1 Letting Go).

2. Love yourself through self-care (see Chapter 2 Giving Yourself Self-Love).

3. Embrace your gratitude attitude as you raise your vibrations even higher
    to manifest what you want and imagine you have already received it
    (see Chapter 3 Let's Start Manifesting).

4. Step into the crystal of your choice
    (see Your Manifestation Crystal Meditation, page 74).

5. Focus on being the director of your own movie
    (see See Your Dreams Come to Life, page 78).

6. Be inspired and smile (see Summoning Inspiration, on page 79, and A Smile
    Can Say More Than A Thousand Words, page 82).

7. Use positive affirmations (see Using Affirmations, page 90).

8. Focus your positive intent.

9. Make a manifestation vision board (see
    page 86).

10. Make a crystal grid (see Manifestation
    Crystal Grids, page 95).

MANIFESTATION: MEETING "THE ONE" OR YOUR SOUL MATE

When your heart is seeking to meet the partner of your dreams it's important to be very focused on what you want and desire. Remember to include everything! The clearer you are the more the universe will give you the love you wish for.

Steps to Manifestation

Your crystal to manifest with: Rose quartz

- Imagine your ideal relationship.

- Visualize the person and how they look.

- How do they make you feel? Do they make you smile and laugh?

- See yourself already with them and how you are together.

- Get excited and feel happy.

- Be in the moment with them, laughing and holding hands.

- Embrace this feeling as though it is happening right now and be grateful for all you have received!

- Write down everything you want from your loved one, such as kindness, romance, passion, connection, friendship, caring, and love.

- Do you want them to have similar hobbies such as keeping fit, going to the gym, jogging, or meditating?

- You can add whatever you want to manifest, including wanting them to be your soul mate.

- If you want them to love children and have babies, write that down.

- The person can be tall or short and have brown or blue eyes, or pink or purple hair. Whatever your heart desires!

- If the connection between you physically, mentally, and spiritually is important, write that down.

MANIFESTATION: YOUR DREAM HOME

The prospect of finding your dream home is so exciting. When you're manifesting the home of your dreams be sure to include everything from the color of the walls to the views from the windows.

Steps to Manifestation

Your crystal to manifest with: Ruby

- Think about all aspects of your dream home.

- Where do you want to live? Be specific about the location.

- Do you want an apartment or a house?

- Picture the front of the house or apartment and what it looks like.

- How many bedrooms?

- How many bathrooms?

- Do you want a walk-in shower?

- Do you want a bath? What style of bath?

- What colors do you want in your new home?

- How do you want your bedroom to look?

- How do you want your kitchen to look? Do you want an island in the center with stools around it or would you like a kitchen table and chairs, or both?

- Describe your living area, down to the size of television, stereo system, etc.

- What type of flooring do you want throughout your home?

- Do you want a big, south-facing garden with a summerhouse and swimming pool or a balcony overlooking the sea? Add every aspect you want. Don't leave anything out!

- See yourself living in your dream home and enjoy how it feels.

- Be grateful for all you are receiving and imagine you are already living there.

- Keep believing and stay focused on finding the dream home for you. You'll know when it is the right one for you.

MANIFESTATION: A NEW CAR

As you begin your journey to manifest a new car, imagine driving it and feeling how it feels. See yourself in it and feel how proud you are having the car you have wanted for so long!

Steps to Manifestation

Your crystal to manifest with: Aquamarine

- What model car? Is it a convertible, sports car, SUV (sport utility vehicle), a 4 x 4, hatchback, coupe, station wagon (estate), sedan (saloon)?

- What are your needs for a car?

- Is it for practical purposes like driving to work and back, helping family members, taking children to school and for play dates? Or is it for your own leisure and indulgence?

- Do you want a car with gears or an automatic?

- Are you dreaming of a hybrid or electric car?

- What color would you like?

- Do you want leather or do you prefer fabric seats?

- Heated seats?

- Electric roof?

- Think about your needs and write down every detail you want from a car.

- Remember how powerful your manifestation vision board is and everything else you are combining with your visualizations.

- Be grateful for receiving the car of your dreams as though you have it already!

When you apply all the elements to manifest your everything, the results are magical! Focus, Believe, and Trust in the Universe.

MANIFESTATION: A NEW JOB

When it's time to find a new job that makes you happy, focus on how the type of job will give you what you need. Don't settle for any job. You can manifest the one you dream about. The right job in the right place with the right people is waiting for you. You can manifest it and anything you want to!

Steps to Manifestation

Your crystal to manifest with: Pyrite

- Focus on positive affirmations—write down what yours are such as "I feel excited to get the job of my dreams" or "I feel confident, happy, and ready to make it happen" (see affirmations, page 90).

- Trust in yourself and your intuition.

- Spend time putting together a manifestation vision board with photos and words on it that represent the job you wish for.

- Write down everything you want from a new job. The type of job, the people you work with—maybe you want them to be friendly and caring.

- As the director and producer of the movie in your mind see yourself in your dream job, feeling happy and content and interacting with lovely colleagues.

- Before your interview, anchor a moment when you felt confident and positive.

- Tell yourself "I can do this!"

- BELIEVE IN YOU.

Be clear about what you want and trust and believe that you can achieve all your dreams.

MANIFESTATION: YOUR DREAM VACATION

If you haven't had the opportunity to go on your dream vacation and you think about it often, I suggest letting the universe know where you want to go and all you wish for from a fabulous vacation. Remember this is the vacation you've always wanted, so include everything!

Steps to Manifestation

Your crystal to manifest with: Turquoise

- Let your pictures do the talking for you on your manifestation vision board!

- Now write down what type of a dream vacation you want. A beautiful beach vacation on an island far away or a city break having fun exploring a city you've always dreamed of visiting? Perhaps you want an adventure vacation, such as climbing Machu Picchu in Peru or visiting or climbing the Virunga mountains in Rwanda to see the gorillas. Whatever you want, be clear with your message.

- Who do you want to go with?

- How long do you want to go for?

- What type of hotel room are you dreaming of? Would you like to walk out of your room onto a porch and sit with your feet in a clear, bright blue sea and watch the tropical fish swim by or do you want amazing views of a city of your dreams?

- Do you imagine lying by a stunning swimming pool on a luxurious lounge chair (sun lounger), feeling the hot sun on your body and being served drinks and food whenever you want?

- Do you see yourself buying the plane tickets or perhaps you're driving to your special place or going on a cruise? Can you see yourself shopping for clothes, planning your outfits, and packing?

- Be grateful for what you are receiving and see yourself on your dream vacation as though it is happening.

OTHER WISHES AND DREAMS

Here are a few ideas for other manifestations that you can personalize so they are unique to you. Spaces have been provided for you to write down a checklist of what you're hoping to manifest in your wish or dream. I have also suggested a suitable crystal for you to hold and keep by your side to enhance your manifestation process.

Manifestation: For Success

Crystal to manifest with: Aventurine

Checklist:

....

....

....

....

....

Manifestation: For Abundance

Crystal to manifest with: Citrine

Checklist:

....

....

....

....

....

....

Manifestation: For Confidence

Crystal to manifest with: Crazy lace agate

Checklist:

....

....

....

....

....

Manifestation: For the Courage to Speak Up

Crystal to manifest with: Kyanite

Checklist:

....

....

....

....

....

Manifestation: For Good health

Crystal to manifest with: Clear quartz

Checklist:

....

....

....

....

....

Manifestation: For Good Grades and Focus for Exams

Crystal to manifest with: Fluorite

Checklist:

....

....

....

....

....

Manifestation: For Manifesting a Pet

Crystal to manifest with: Lapis lazuli

Checklist:

....

....

....

....

Manifestation: To Be More Creative

Crystal to manifest with: Carnelian

Checklist:

....

....

....

....

....

IN SUMMARY: Tips to Remember

1. Play music that makes you feel good—dancing is also a great way to lift your mood!

2. Focus on positive affirmations.

3. Keep your positive wishes and affirmations jar nearby and remember all the good things you want to manifest in your life.

4. Look at your manifestation vision board every day.

5. Let your manifestation crystal grid work for you. Leave it in a safe place to send your positive wishes to the universe.

6. Be patient and stay focused, positive, and hopeful. What you are wishing for will happen when you're ready to receive and free from what's been holding you back.

YOUR GUIDE TO MANIFESTING

Focus on your dreams.

Open your heart to embrace everything you are ready to receive.

Remember what you can achieve.

Be grateful for all you have received before you have it.

Feel your inner peace.

Visualize all you dream of.

Have empathy and understanding for yourself.

Nurture yourself by focusing on your self-care.

Embrace your future and the freedom you feel.

Smile and keep smiling!

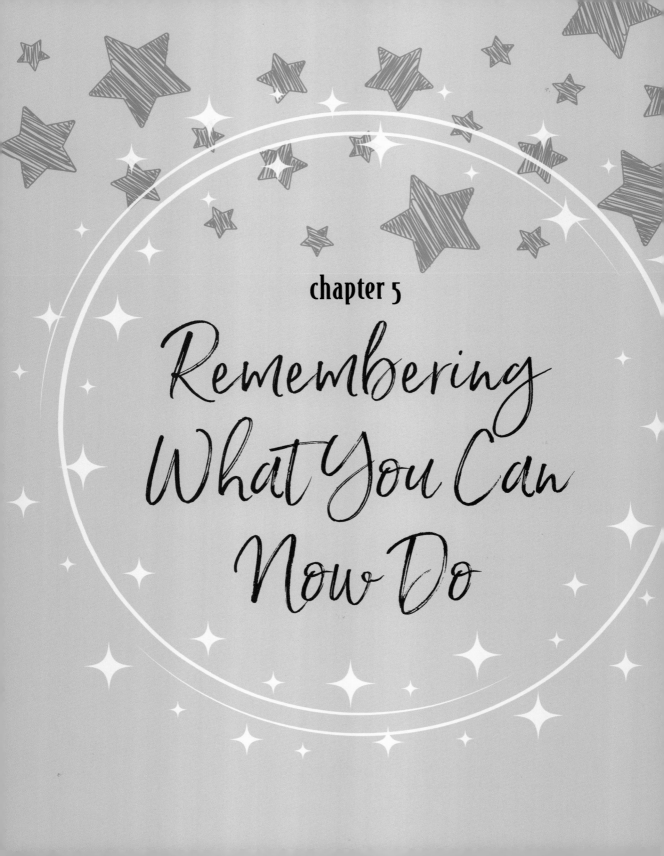

chapter 5

Remembering What You Can Now Do

Working through your "Manifest Your Everything" journey, from letting go and loving yourself to manifesting your dreams, is a powerful process. Investing time and energy in creating the life you want requires care and attention. It is a work in progress.

This final chapter reflects on key aspects of the book you've been working through so far. There are other topics for you to explore too, including exercise, healthy eating, and the importance of checking in with yourself regularly to focus on your self-care physically, mentally, and spiritually.

Keep revisiting what you have done in previous chapters. You may need to go through the process again. It is like peeling away the layers of an onion—there may be lots of layers to remove until you can finally wave goodbye to everything that has been a heavy burden in your life. Then you are ready to manifest your everything and all you wish for.

When you're used to a fast pace of life the power of stillness when you meditate and slow down can be daunting. But if you keep practicing, it becomes part of you and your everyday life. Please remember to focus on the "three R's"—Release, Renew, and Receive—and follow the Manifest Your Everything processes as you travel on your special journey. Loving yourself will open your heart to so much and life will once again be full of happiness and joy.

Keep Your Confidence Shining Through

When you feel confident, peaceful, and happy within, you are ready to manifest everything you wish for. Only you can choose what you do and how you do it. You are in control and that's a wonderful feeling. When you let go of negative situations and the people who hurt you, your self-esteem, self-worth, and self-belief will return. Remember:

- Never let anyone make you doubt yourself again.

- Never let anyone put you down.

- Never let anyone tell you what you can't do.

You can do anything you want because you are unique and special! Love yourself, let everything else flow, and magic will happen! Keep reminding yourself how important it is to:

- Believe in yourself.

- Trust in you.

- Choose what you want to do.

DEALING WITH HURT AND FINDING HOPE IN YOUR HEART

When you've been hurt by a loved one, it can take time to believe that there really is true love out in the world. Maybe a friend or situation has also knocked your self-esteem and belief in yourself. Whatever it is, be patient and kind to yourself (see Self-Empathy in a Positive Way, page 132). When you start focusing on "yourself," it's amazing how one day you wake up and recognize that "it's time for positive change." Anything is possible when you have hope in your heart and focus on what you dream of.

It's an enlightening moment when you realize you've let go of the burden and hurt you've carried, and it's suddenly lifted. Embrace the moment and let your confidence shine through. The universe will see this as you feel free and become ready to move forward by loving yourself and manifesting your dreams.

Boost Your Confidence and Keep It Shining!

Giving yourself a boost of confidence can enhance your mood and help you feel so much better. From anchoring your special moment to remembering your gratitude attitude, the list below can give you the boost you may need. (See pages 76 and 62.)

CONFIDENCE BOOSTERS

Here are some confidence boosters to make you feel good and help you manifest your dreams with even more clarity, positive intent, and focus.

- Focus on the NOW.

- Exercise regularly—around three or four times a week.

- Keep repeating your positive affirmations.

- Anchor your special moment of happiness, peace, or calm.

- Remember your achievements and congratulate yourself.

- Be inspired by others, nature, or a place.

- Meditate once or twice a day.

- Keep a crazy lace agate confidence crystal with you.

- Re-evaluate your work–life balance to give you time and space.

- Give yourself the love and care you deserve.

- Spend time with positive people.

- Do something that makes you laugh.

- Smile!

- Remember your gratitude attitude.

- Change your self-perception to a positive one.

Write down three things to give yourself a confidence boost today:

1. ....

2. ....

3. ....

POSITIVE AFFIRMATIONS FOR CONFIDENCE

Here are a few positive affirmations you might like to say to yourself to help build trust and even more confidence in yourself:

- I trust myself.

- I value myself and my feelings.

- I feel confident from within.

- I trust my intuition.

Listening to your intuition can enable you to see, hear, and feel things more clearly.

Once you are in touch with your emotions and feel confident within, you can begin to build more trusting relationships with the right people and manifest your dreams.

"The rule is you have to dance a little bit in the morning before you leave the house because it changes the way you walk out in the world."

Sandra Bullock

Keep a Manifest Your Everything Journal

Keep track of everything you're doing and achieving. Use a daily journal or write in your diary every day as a reminder of how well you are progressing on your journey to achieve your goals and happiness.

Write down in the spaces below three things you are doing to focus on manifesting your dreams. This can be anything from your manifestation vision board (see page 86) to making a crystal grid (see Manifestation Crystal Grids, page 95).

1. ....

2. ....

3. ....

Stopping Negative Influences

If someone enters your life who doesn't serve you, what will you do now that you have the tools to say goodbye and not let negative influences into your life? For a reminder of how to do this, revisit the exercises under Creating Mental Space, on page 16. Say the following out loud or to yourself:

"I'm in control of me, not you."

"This is your issue, not mine."

"I'm taking care of me and you're over there."

Daily Routine for Positive Change

Having a positive routine every morning and evening can ground you and keep you balanced and focused. When you're in a good place mentally, physically, and spiritually, the universe knows, and you'll begin receiving what you asked for. Here are some tips on how to do this:

1. Wake up with a smile!

2. Meditate or say a morning prayer.

3. Shower and let the water flow over your Crown chakra, to awaken your senses and inspire you for the day!

4. Choose invigorating essential oils such as orange, rosemary, cedarwood, and peppermint, to give you a boost.

5. Eat a healthy, well-balanced diet.

6. Sleep for at least 7–8 hours every night.

7. Give yourself a self-healing treatment with your crystals (see Working with Crystals and Chakras, page 46).

8. Make sure to focus on having some "me-time" during your day (see Chapter 2 Giving Yourself Love for suggested techniques and treatments).

The Power of Sleep

A good seven or eight hours of sleep a night is so beneficial to our health, mindset, energy levels, and concentration. Without a good night's sleep, it can be challenging to function normally at home and/or work. The amount of sleep each person needs is different. Obviously, new mothers can be sleep-deprived—having a new baby and being up all hours is exhausting. Thankfully, the first few months are the most challenging until the baby settles into a routine!

If you don't get enough sleep, it eventually catches up with you. If you're working late and have an early schedule, do what you can to re-energize by giving yourself ten minutes to close your eyes, breathe, and relax during the day. Plan to have some sleep catch-up time to avoid burn out.

If the universe sees you are sleep deprived and unable to focus and manage your emotions, it will keep sending you emotions that you don't want as well as feelings of exhaustion.

Refocus on what you can do to ensure you get the right amount of sleep to provide you with the energy you need. Here are some suggestions to help you get a good night's sleep if you're struggling:

- Hold a malachite crystal for an hour before you go to sleep and then take it to bed with you. Put it under your pillow, keep holding it, or place it on your nightstand. I recommend blue calcite for children.

- Meditate for an hour or less before going to sleep. You can hold your crystal when you do this. (See Release Inner Turmoil through Meditation, on page 21, for guidance on meditating.)

- Avoid caffeine for at least 4–6 hours before you go to bed.

- Turn off your phone and/or computer as these can keep you awake. Turning them off will also help you to avoid the electromagnetic fog you can receive from them. Fluorite is a wonderful crystal to keep by your computer and phone during the day to combat this.

- Use essential oils in a diffuser and/or have a lavender pillow next to you. Relax in a soothing crystal and essential oil bath (see Amanda's Amethyst Crystal and Lavender Oil Recipe, page 53). Always use caution with essential oils.

Healthy Balanced Eating

Loving yourself and letting go of negative emotions enables you to take control of situations that may have sent you into a spiral in the past. Cleansing your mind and body with the exercises you've been doing in this book will give you the peace and power from within to manifest your everything.

Healthy eating is part of this cleansing process. It's fine to have the occasional treat and enjoy a piece of cake, a chocolate bar, or an ice cream. But if you do this every day, then that's when your body will cry out for you to STOP having sugar splurges and instead give it healthy food and a well-balanced diet. If you don't look after your body, your energy levels can drop and you may put on weight, which can increase your risk of health problems such as heart issues, cancer, and diabetes. Sugary snacks may taste delicious, but they won't benefit you if you eat them regularly. Letting go of everything that doesn't serve you includes saying goodbye to overindulging your body with an unhealthy diet. I have always believed in having "everything in moderation."

Many people blame their bad eating habits on not having the time to make healthy meals and they end up eating "junk" food because they feel they're just too busy to cook. Others blame their circumstances and use "emotional eating." This is easily done, especially if you are not in control of yourself and your emotions.

However, when you say goodbye to excuses like "I can't stop," you will feel the benefits of "I can" and "I'm going to." Put an inspirational note on your fridge door or anywhere else you'll see it regularly to inspire you—say something like "I'm So Proud of You! You Can Do This!" This is a positive message that the universe will hear. Believe what you tell yourself, live it every day, and embrace the power of the universe and how adjusting your inner dialogue will change your life and give you what you wish for.

AVOIDING OVERINDULGENCE

Here's a few suggestions to help you resist moments of overindulgence:

- Drink plenty of water to avoid misreading signs of thirst for hunger.

- Tell the emotional you: "I'M IN CONTROL OF YOU, YOU'RE NOT IN CONTROL OF ME."

- Every time you're tempted to eat an indulgent treat, imagine mixing it with something you absolutely hate! I'm not a fan of anchovies. Imagining them mixed in with my favorite chocolate bar stops me eating it! I opt for the healthy options of freshly chopped vegetables or berries instead.

- Focus your energy on other distractions such as taking a break in the fresh air, calling a friend, or changing your mindset by working on something different and coming back to what's frustrating you later!

- Hold an appatite crystal or wear it as a bracelet or necklace, as appatite can help reduce hunger. Hold the crystal for two minutes before you want to eat anything. Keep doing it! The chocolate cookies may still be in the cupboard in a few weeks' time!

The Power of Exercise

Like healthy eating, exercise has a huge part to play in helping you to manifest your positive dreams. Your health and well-being, both mentally and physically, are the key to feeling good. Without good nutrition and exercise you won't be giving yourself everything you need to take care of you.

MAKE THE MOST OF NATURAL FEEL-GOOD CHEMICALS

When we exercise, our bodies release chemicals called endorphins which give us the feel-good factor. This is a great excuse to exercise and it's an amazing feeling. The good news is that you can give yourself a feel-good endorphin boost any time you want—it's your choice when. So, look for ways you can include exercise, along with a healthy eating regime, into your lifestyle, so you can feel even better. If you're already doing this, that's brilliant! You're halfway there to focusing on manifesting your everything.

Regular exercise three or four times a week is beneficial in so many ways to your health and mental well-being. For example, it helps to release stress, boosts your energy levels, and lifts your mood if you're feeling low. It can also help lower blood pressure and has so many other amazing health benefits. **Always seek professional advice before starting an exercise regime if you have a medical condition.**

"Lack of activity destroys the good condition of
every human being, while movement
and methodical physical exercise save it
and preserve it."

Plato

There are many options for keeping fit, including going to the gym, doing different workout classes such as Zumba, hip-hop, and other dance classes, spin, bar classes, aqua aerobics, conditioning classes, boot camp, boxing, and circuit classes. Other alternatives include Pilates and different types of yoga, including hot yoga and power yoga. The list is endless and there are classes suitable for all levels.

Tai chi, chi kung, and other physical meditation practices are also the ideal way to start your day with a clear mind and focus.

Exercising outdoors means you also benefit from being in nature, enjoying the beauty and fresh air whatever the weather. Brisk walking, jogging, running, or hiking in the mountains or countryside may be something you'd like to do. There is so much choice!

If it's your first time going to the gym or exercising outdoors, start slowly and build up gradually. Ask the advice of a professional trainer in your area or a fitness instructor who teaches classes. Avoid overdoing things when you first start! Remember to:

• Never embark on an exercise routine without warming up and stretching your muscles first. The last thing you want is a torn calf muscle or hamstring. So, aim to have a 10-minute warmup and stretch before starting any exercise such as running. Perhaps you could go on a brisk walk for 10 minutes first. Also make sure to learn how to warm up and stretch correctly. If you're in a workout class at the gym, they should always start with a warmup and stretch.

• Stretch after exercising to warm down and always drink plenty of water to keep your body hydrated.

FINDING MOTIVATION

Joining a class with other people can give you the motivation you may need. You could also ask a friend to meet up for regular nature walks or runs. This is a good way to commit to getting fit as neither of you will want to let the other down. Whatever you decide to do, remember that exercise is one of the paths to taking care of you and feeling positive and energized, and it helps you to focus on manifesting what you want.

CASE STUDY: Mandy's Story

During an outdoor session with Mandy, we began by talking and walking as she described how anxious she'd been feeling. As we walked, I quickened our pace and gave her some tips—including to focus on the beauty around her. This helped release her anxiety. She began projecting more energy in her voice and body language. Mandy said she felt calmer and happier than she had for the past six months.

If you're not feeling a boost of energy when you walk, quicken the pace or break into a jog or run, which will encourage a release of more endorphins. When a runner wins a race, you can see the feel-good factor on their face! It's known as "runners' natural high."

DANCE! DANCE! DANCE!

When was the last time you heard a song you loved and just danced to it? Every time I hear Pharrell Williams sing "Happy," I want to dance, sing along, and clap because it makes me feel so happy! Whatever type of music you love, from rock to pop or country music, it has so many benefits, whether you're dancing alone at home or at a nightclub. These include helping to relieve stress and giving you a boost if you're feeling low.

Dancing is also a great form of exercise and can help improve your aerobic fitness and increase your energy levels, along with many more health benefits. When you dance, you feel good, and when you feel good, you are ready to manifest your everything because you're in a good place and space in your mind.

SINGING IN THE SHOWER!

Have you ever noticed how much better you feel after enjoying an invigorating shower and singing your way through the whole thing! You may not be Lady Gaga or Adam Lambert, but that's okay! Singing along at the top of your voice or quietly to yourself can give you a wonderful mindset boost, release stress, and set you up for the day, among other health benefits! Another wonderful benefit of singing in the shower is you're sending the universe a tuneful message that you're feeling good!

The Power of Self-Encouragement

Giving yourself encouragement can enhance your confidence and help you feel better about yourself. It can also enable you to keep going and believe in your achievements and what you can do. This is another positive message you can send to the universe. The more encouragement you give yourself, the more the universe will hear you and keep sending you more as you manifest what you wish for.

The Olympic champion sprinter Usain Bolt adopted a powerfully positive pose: pointing dramatically to the sky every time he won a race.

"The sky has no limits," he said, **"neither should you."** He also said: **"I know what I can do, so I never doubt myself."** Self-encouragement was Usain's thing—it can also be yours. It's simply focusing on what you have achieved and can achieve.

Encouragement also comes when you surround yourself with positive people who care, and you are grateful to those who have encouraged and supported you. Here are a few tips for finding encouragement:

- Start your own "Encouragement File" of achievements. Record positive comments from others and write down things that make you smile and laugh.

- Use positive language to reinforce others. Saying things such as "That was fabulous" often results in you getting something positive back.

- Give yourself words of encouragement such as "I'm proud of you."

Imagine stepping into Usain Bolt's shoes. What pose and words of encouragement would you adopt? See Summoning Inspiration, on page 79, for more ideas for finding inspiration.

Self-Empathy in a Positive Way

Developing self-empathy helps you to recognize your own unspoken emotions. Feeling empathy and compassion for yourself also helps you understand these emotions—and to see, hear, and feel the needs of others. Having empathy for ourselves gives us the power to understand ourselves and others even more.

Emotional self-awareness can enhance your belief in yourself and give you the strength to manage challenges. If you are too self-critical, you will reinforce negative beliefs, and when you have negative thoughts, the universe will send you what you are focusing on.

If your inner dialogue is full of criticism, then your conversations with others may also be too negative. Do you ever catch yourself thinking the following:

- I need to be tougher on myself.

- Why can't I do better?

- I blame myself.

Changing your inner dialogue to one of self-empathy and compassion helps you to say things to yourself and others in a kinder, more empathetic, and compassionate way (see Reframing Negative Thoughts and Choosing Positive Ones, page 70).

POSITIVE SELF-TALK

Write down three things you can tell yourself that are kind, caring, and understanding and show compassion and empathy.

1. ....

2. ....

3. ....

Protecting Yourself

It is very important to protect yourself from negative influences (see page 16), especially if you're working with somebody who doesn't have your best interests at heart or if you're in a toxic relationship. This exercise will also give you protection wherever you go and whoever you are with if needed.

EXERCISE: Create a Colored Bubble of Protective Light

This exercise will provide you with a beautiful protective bubble that you can visualize around you whenever you go out and/or feel you need to protect yourself.

1. Choose a color, such as gold, to be your protective light, then close your eyes.

2. Take a slow, deep breath in through your nose and then breathe out slowly through your mouth. Repeat this three times.

3. Imagine your colored light shining brightly from within you. Feel its warmth and see the light glow inside your mind and body.

4. Now see your light spill out from the top of your head and surround you like a golden shower.

5. See your protective bubble of light all around you. See its magnificent color and light shining brightly.

6. Feel the flow of the light protecting you from any outside negative influences.

7. Anchor this moment (see Anchoring, page 76).

8. Every time you want to protect yourself with your colored bubble of light, you can also use your anchor.

"If your compassion does not include yourself, it is incomplete."

Jack Kornfield

Reboot the Computer of Your Mind

When you've let go of what you don't want and it no longer serves you, your perception of yourself changes to become more positive and focused. Your outlook on life shifts because you're embracing everything instead of running away from it.

Sometimes you may need to give yourself a reboot and readjust a few things if anything has become overwhelming. I like to look at the human mind as a computer! I use this analogy to give you a greater understanding of yourself and how there may be occasions when you need to reboot the computer of your mind.

The wonderful thing about your brain is that it has an amazing elasticity and ability to reboot. When a computer is overloaded and the colored ball starts spinning, you may need to shut it down to reboot it—clearing what's stalling it and starting again. It's the same with the computer of your mind when there's change, confusion, or overload.

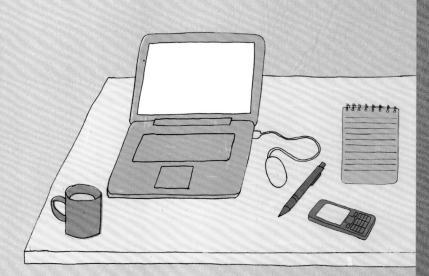

EXERCISE: **Breathe Your Way to Calm and Relaxation**

Scott was facing challenges with his work–life balance and his energy levels were very low. He had a hectic work schedule and a one-month-old baby. Scott felt exhausted, stressed, and overloaded. When he came to see me, the first thing I suggested he do was to STOP and BREATHE, so he could begin to reboot.

Breathing can help you to relax and feel calmer. It brings you back into focus, enabling you to concentrate and feel more in control. Use this simple breathing exercise if you think you need to relax, refocus, and reboot.

1. Close your eyes, then take a slow, deep breath in through your nose and, as you do so, let your shoulders lift up to your ears. Hold for 2–4 seconds.

2. Release and breathe out slowly through your mouth as your shoulders drop and your mind and body start to relax.

3. Repeat this three times and return to your normal breathing. Notice how much more relaxed and calm you now feel.

4. Every time you feel stressed or overwhelmed, STOP, BREATHE, RELAX. Repeat this a few times during the day as part of your daily routine to help you stay in a calm and peaceful place in your mind.

Here are some extra reboot tips:

- Focus on exercises to quieten your mind and alleviate stress such as tai chi, meditation, breathwork, and nature walks.

- Change your routine and give yourself some "me-time" during the day. Try switching off your phone and computer for 20–30 minutes to give your brain a rest! This will help rebalance your mind and give you the headspace to RELAX, REFRESH, AND REVITILIZE. Do this before you go to sleep too—it works wonders! Staying on your phone or computer before going to sleep doesn't give you time to switch off and calm yourself.

- Have some fun!

- Go for a walk in nature or anywhere outside in the city during the day, even if it's raining! Fresh air gives your metabolism a boost. Getting wet if it's raining can be invigorating. You can use an umbrella and pretend you are Gene Kelly in the movie *Singing in the Rain*!

How a Treat Day Can Give Your Mindset a Boost

Are you making time for a regular "treat day"? Give yourself a special day to relax and do the things you love, such as meeting up with friends, seeing a movie, or having fun at a workout class like hip-hop or Zumba! Do what makes you happy and give yourself a mindset boost.

One of my clients, Sammy, is a great example of why taking time for yourself is so important. Sammy is a lawyer who was worried that her business would collapse if she wasn't always available. She wasn't creating boundaries and had no "me-time" activities in her schedule.

Sammy worked long hours every day until overwhelm kicked in physically and mentally. Then she had to stop and rest. That was when she reached out and asked me for help. Sammy worked through the "Manifest Your Everything" process and realized how much she had been holding onto things that were detrimental to herself.

We also looked at various ways Sammy could give herself a "treat day" each week to help her relax, refresh, and re-energize. She started to give herself the care she needed and manifest what she really wanted, which was time to enjoy life instead of being afraid to slow down and stop. Here are some areas I worked on with Sammy:

- Putting time in your diary to give you more headspace.

- Giving yourself the weekend off or having your weekend during the week.

- Doing something special for you.

Taking care of your needs is a priority, as this will enable you to be more productive, feel calm and relaxed, and send out your positive intentions to the universe. For more guidance on this, see What Are You Doing To Take Care of Yourself?, on page 42, and work with your Circle of Self-Care.

Following her "Manifest Your Everything" journey, Sammy decided to do what she had always wanted and changed her job. She loved exercising and doing classes, and she had always dreamed of teaching keep-fit. Her family thought she was crazy to give up all she had achieved. But Sammy has never been happier! She teaches classes at a health club on weekends and one night a week. Sammy is now a consultant at a law firm three days a week and loving her new life!

What's important in life to you now that you've manifested your everything? Are you ready to live your dream life?

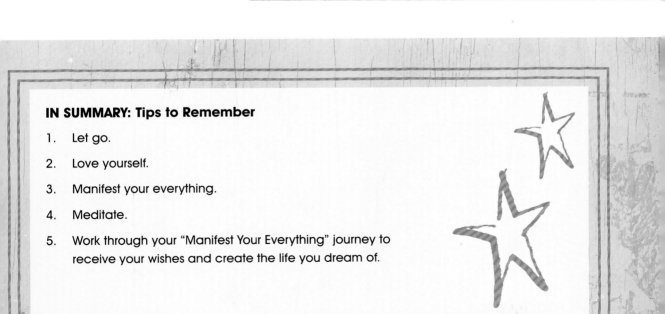

IN SUMMARY: Tips to Remember

1. Let go.

2. Love yourself.

3. Manifest your everything.

4. Meditate.

5. Work through your "Manifest Your Everything" journey to receive your wishes and create the life you dream of.

LOVING YOURSELF AND MANIFESTING WHAT YOU WANT

Although you are now reading the last part of the book, having revisited different areas of your "Manifesting Your Everything" journey and looked at new topics to embrace such as exercise, healthy eating, and self-encouragement, this is not where your journey ends. This moment marks a brand-new and exciting beginning, as you welcome the new, positively focused you who is now giving yourself the love you deserve to manifest your dreams.

When you manifest what you wish for from the universe, be grateful, be happy, and be proud of what you have achieved. Imagine you have already received your wishes. The more positive, confident, and excited you are about life, the more you will receive what you are feeling. Give yourself a "hug of love" (see page 66) and recognize how far you've come. Love yourself, be kind to yourself, and the magic of manifesting will happen.

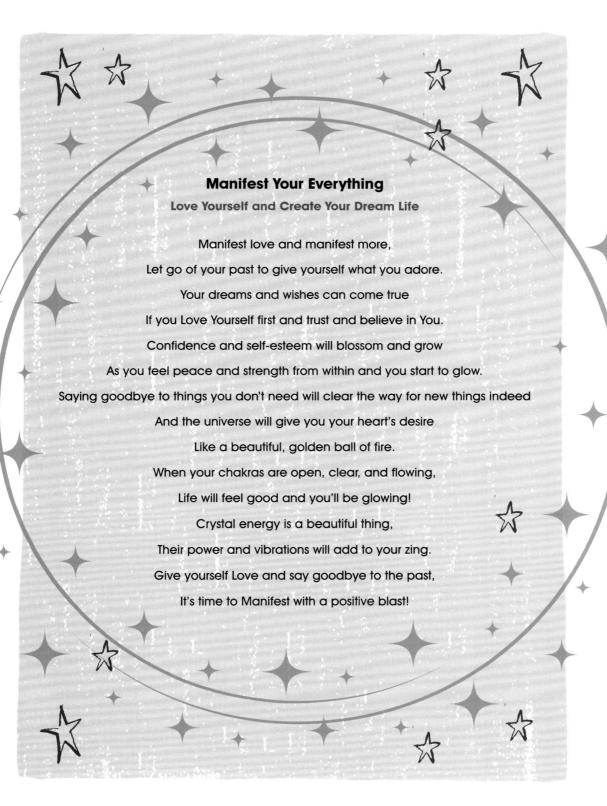

Manifest Your Everything

Love Yourself and Create Your Dream Life

Manifest love and manifest more,

Let go of your past to give yourself what you adore.

Your dreams and wishes can come true

If you Love Yourself first and trust and believe in You.

Confidence and self-esteem will blossom and grow

As you feel peace and strength from within and you start to glow.

Saying goodbye to things you don't need will clear the way for new things indeed

And the universe will give you your heart's desire

Like a beautiful, golden ball of fire.

When your chakras are open, clear, and flowing,

Life will feel good and you'll be glowing!

Crystal energy is a beautiful thing,

Their power and vibrations will add to your zing.

Give yourself Love and say goodbye to the past,

It's time to Manifest with a positive blast!

Final Words

While writing Chapter 4 of this book, I was accompanied by the wonderful music for the "Platinum Party at the Palace" on television to celebrate Queen Elizabeth II's Platinum Jubilee. It was inspiring, magical, and uplifting, and I sang along! Queen, Craig David, Alicia Keys, Rod Stewart, Andrew Lloyd Webber, Andrea Bocelli, and the fabulous Diana Ross for the finale were all incredible! These were just some of the amazing artists playing at the concert as I wrote *Manifest Your Everything*! I'm sure this contributed to the powerful Chapter 4 Your Messages to the Universe!

Since I first wrote this, our beautiful, inspirational Queen has passed. She will always be remembered for the amazing lady she was.

MY LOVE AND HOPE FOR YOU

Now you've been on your journey to manifest your everything by letting go of what no longer serves you and learning to love yourself and create your dream life, my wish for you is to find love, peace, happiness, and abundance. May your dreams become your reality. I send you love, laughter, hope, and belief forever in your heart.

Give yourself what you need. Your love, your time, and your care. Continue to manifest your everything and magic will happen!

Nicci xx

Cleansing Crystals

Throughout your "Manifest Your Everything" journey you've been working with the powerful energy of crystals. If you notice that a crystal is lacking in luster or not as sparkly as usual, this means it needs cleansing. Cleansing is different to cleaning. Cleaning involves washing a crystal, as you would wash your hands. Cleansing is spiritual and gives crystals back their sparkle, so they can work to their full potential. There are different ways to cleanse crystals. Here are some options for cleansing crystals and giving them back their sparkle:

1. Give crystals a bubble bath in some good-quality dishwashing liquid. You can almost hear them squealing with joy! Place them in a colander and run them under tepid water for about a minute to rinse. Alternatively, you can just run them under tepid water for about a minute.

2. Put your crystals outside or inside on a windowsill when there is a full or new moon to allow the lunar energy to cleanse your crystals.

3. Burn some frankincense or sandalwood, or you can use incense sticks which are an easy way of doing it and allow the fragrant smoke to cleanse the crystals.

4. Bury your crystals in the earth and leave them for 24 hours. When you take them out, run them under tepid water. Your crystals have literally enjoyed a rebirth. It's a lovely thing to do. Be careful if you have a dog or cat, as they may want to dig the crystals up. If you live in an apartment and don't have access to a backyard, put some earth in a dish and bury your crystals inside. It's exactly the same process.

5. Smudge your crystals to cleanse them (see The Smudging Ceremony, page 31).

Please note: Crystals like malachite and bumble bee jasper should not be put in water—malachite can leach copper and bumble bee jasper contains arsenic. Neither are suitable for children to handle. The other crystals referenced in the book can all be put under running water.

Index

Acknowledgments

There are so many people I want to say thank you to, including my fabulous students and clients who continue to inspire me as I see the positive changes in them as they move forward on their journey.

Thank you to my wonderful family and friends for your constant belief in me, especially my parents, son and daughter Adam and Gemma, my daughter-in-law Emma and son-in-law Adam, niece Katie Kit Kat, nephew Jason, and my sister and brother-in-law, Boo and Keith.

A huge thank you for the massive support from Monika and Tibor Kolb. You are both so awesome! I love your energy and enthusiasm for all you do in the fitness world and beyond!

Thank you so much to my brilliant hairdresser James Demetris, the best hair colorist Zoe Jacobson, and amazing beautician Xenia Capsalis. Your support has been incredible and you all give so much to so many and are so caring.

Shenel Eray thank you for the beautiful love yourself potions and affirmation jars for my "Love Yourself and Manifest Your Dreams" workshops. Everyone loves them, including me!

To my amazing partner Philip. Thank you for being you and my incredibly wonderful partner forever encouraging me to do even more!! Your love and belief in me is so special. Teddy and Honey, our amazing puppies, I adore you!

Thank you to my beautiful grandsons Louis, Charlie, Toby, and Jack, you bring sunshine and smiles into my heart every day and make it shine with happiness.

I feel very blessed and am so grateful to have you all in my life. Thank you.

Love you all.

Nicci xx